Should earth against my soul engage,
And fiery darts be hurled,
Then I can smile at Satan's rage
And face a frowning world.

— WHEN I CAN READ MY TITLE CLEAR

Published by DayStar Publishing
P.O. Box 464
Miamitown, Ohio 45041
www.daystarpublishing.org

ISBN: 978-1-890120-99-3
LOCN: 2015938425

Cover and maps were created by Truth and Song Christian Bookstore. www.truthandsong.com

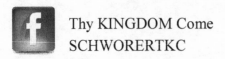
Thy KINGDOM Come
SCHWORERTKC

Thy KINGDOM Come

The Shadow of the King

By Rick Schworer

Note to reader: while the overall story of the kingdom of heaven is true, this is a work of fiction based upon the author's interpretation of the Bible and history. Additionally this is not an attempt to breathe life into the Scriptures but rather to demonstrate that the Bible is the most amazing book ever written. May God bless you while you study these things out for yourself.

Other than the cover and maps, all images are public domain and are used for their classical and timeless value; they are not necessarily the author's impression of what these characters or events appeared as.

In this book the story of the kingdom begins to shifts from the physical to the spiritual. It is the battles of prayer, repentance, holiness, separation, and the consecration of the people that decide their fate. For that reason I've chosen to dedicate this book to my wife, Melissa, who has stood by me and inspired me in these areas like few others.

Introduction

I hope you enjoy this dramatized retelling of the story of the kingdom of heaven.

This is not the story of the whole Bible. This is not the story of the kingdom of God; that's a spiritual kingdom based on spiritual warfare. This story, in its essence, is not even the story of redemption that we all know and love, though that plays a major part. This is the story of a physical and earthly kingdom that by and large has been won and lost by physical and earthly warfare.

This story is about flawed human beings throughout history that God used in mighty ways. These individuals all had their highs and lows; they all had times of failure and valor. But just as this story is about people, it's also about the hope they all possessed.

This is a story on authority. This story is about a King and a kingdom that primarily pertains to one of the bloodiest chunks of ground the world has ever known: Israel.

This is the story of a promise, which is as of yet unfulfilled and was given roughly six thousand years ago to two guilty people who stood trembling before

God; a promise about the day in which the serpent's head would be bruised.

That promise has meant different things to different people throughout history, and it's had a few other promises come along with it: namely, three hundred thousand square miles of land in the Middle East.

Between God and Satan lies the will of a group of people who will either accept the kingdom and its requirements or suffer the consequences. Voyage through time as Satan attempts to stop or stall the fulfillment of the Garden Promise and his own eternal reckoning.

Rest assured, the King will come and will bring with him the final consummation of the kingdom, and when he does it will be a kingdom of peace. Until that day expect war and mayhem, religion and faith, betrayal and treachery. Until his kingdom comes and his will is done on Earth as it is in Heaven, we live under a curse.

Even so, come, Lord Jesus.

TABLE OF CONTENTS

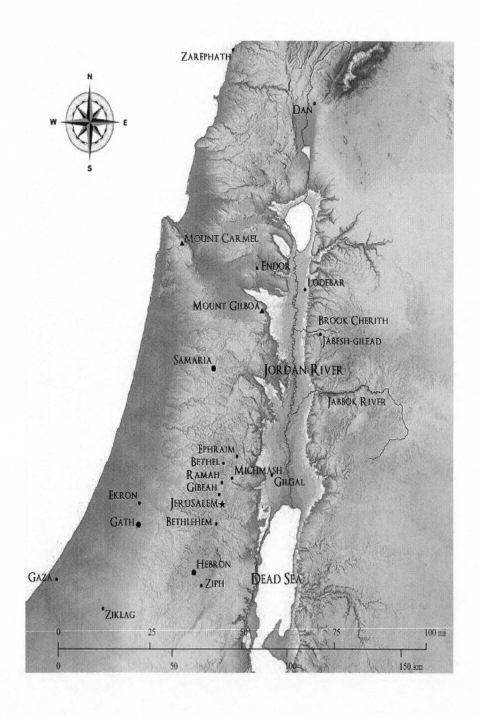

Chapter One

"I will be thy king: where *is any other* that may save thee in all thy cities? and thy judges of whom thou saidst, Give me a king and princes?
I gave thee a king in mine anger, and took *him* away in my wrath."
Hosea 13:10-11

1095 B.C. Ramah

The kingdom had not come.

Though the people of the promise had dwelt in the land given to Moses for nearly three hundred years, they hadn't come close to taking what was promised to Abraham. They had no king, but operated under a theocratic rule governed by judges and priests. The seed had not arrived. Though they were a nation they hardly thought of themselves as such, operating more as a loosely formed confederation of tribes than anything else.

With enemies on every side, they shouldn't have survived. From a human standpoint, such a disorganized group of people with virtually no central government should be easy to overrun, and when God wasn't with them, they were.

And like humans do when a solution to a problem seems to be there for the grabbing and doesn't involve faith, they decided they needed the central rule that a king would give them. They reasoned that with the constant Philistine threat looming over them the best solution was to organize their way out of the dilemma.

In a small room, dimly lit by a candle, we rejoin our story with a gray haired man crying out on his face before God.

"LORD, if you allow them do this there's going to be disaster. This can't be the right way. There's no security to be had in a king!"

"Samuel," the LORD said. "They're not rejecting you, they're rejecting me."

"LORD, they're setting themselves up for a disaster. They've had a hard enough time as it is, but they've always been delivered by judges with a heart for you. What happens when their rulers, the people that are supposed to lead them, want nothing to do with you? What happens when generation after generation of kings are wicked?"

The LORD spoke softly to the prophet. "Samuel, let them have their king. But make sure they know what they're getting."

* * *

Standing before the people Samuel let them have it. "The LORD has granted your request for a king."

Before the excited crowd could respond he held up his hand and continued to speak. "But let me tell what this king is going to be like. If you like your freedoms, that's too bad because you're going to be losing a lot of them.

"If you like the fact that we only go to war when we have to, that's also too bad. Hearken unto me, O house of Israel, when you set a king over you, you're asking for war. A man with too much power only wants more power. A king is going to be looking for every chance he can to grow his kingdom – that's what they do!"

The crowd erupted. "The glory of Israel! God save the king for the glory of Israel!"

Samuel scolded them. "You fools! This king is going to take your boys away from working your farms to grow his power! You're not going to have a choice! Your young men are going to leave their homes defenseless and shed their blood for what? For more dirt? For more land? You'd sacrifice the best among you for a bowl of red pottage?"

Samuel took a deep breath. "He's going to take your sons and your daughters. Your daughters will serve as cooks and bakers. He's going to take your food to feed his armies. Your vineyards will be his. Your property will be his. He's going to be a raiser of taxes.

"In that day you're going to cry out because of your king, but there's no going back."

Someone stepped out from the crowd. "Look Samuel, we appreciate everything you've done for us throughout the years, but you have to understand that the Philistine problem isn't going to go away. They already have garrisons in areas of Israel that they don't belong in. What's next, a full scale invasion? We need a king to go out before us and fight our battles for us."

"The LORD is giving you your king," Samuel said.

Not many days later, a young man by the name of Saul knelt before the prophet as the vial of oil was dumped on his head. The first king of Israel had been anointed.

Saul was a unique man. He was reluctant to take the power given to him, and from all outward appearances he was a humble man. He was tall and strong, his visual appearance alone commanded respect. The people were exuberant, and in the days to follow Saul's courage and heroism would be on full display.

God had chosen for them a mighty man of valour.

Chapter Two

"And the Spirit of the LORD will come upon thee, and
thou shalt prophesy with them, and shalt be turned into
another man."
I Samuel 10:6

Not long after in Jabesh-Gilead

The doors to the governor's hall swung open
and six men walked in as if they owned the
place. They were nomadic Ammonite
warriors, brutal, heartless and cocky; they would just as
soon gut a person as talk to him. At this particular
moment, they had the Jewish town of Jabesh-Gilead
surrounded.

"Governor, your town is mine," Nahash said.

"Why are you here? What is it you want?"

"Anything and everything we can carry off with us."

The governor raised his hands. "Well, it's yours!
Take what you need, just spare us!"

Nahash winced, as if disappointed. "No, no. . . it's
not going to be that easy. Here's what's going to happen:
you are going to allow us to take whatever we want, of
course, but if you want to live you're also going to let us
remove the right eye of every man, woman, and child in
this town."

The ruler of the city gasped. "That's terrible, what
would be the point of that? Why would you be so
cruel?"

"Oh, I don't know," Nahash said as he paced the floor. "I just like the missing eye look, the eye patch look. It's big in Syria right now. There's just something about the right eye being utterly darkened that I. . ."

In one smooth movement the renegade drew his sword and brought it around and down towards one of his men. The man blocked it with a small buckler he had in his right hand.

Nahash gave the man a smile and look of approval, and then returned the sword. He drew a small blade in its place and placed the tip of it on the right cheekbone of the Jewish leader.

"You see," Nahash said dryly as his foul breath pierced the man's senses, "that man would have died if he was missing his right eye. He wouldn't have seen that coming, and he couldn't have blocked it. I don't want to kill everyone here; I'm going to need to come back time and time again. I just don't want to take the chance that later on I'm going to have the hassle of fighting an armed militia."

The governor dug deep to find the courage and the words. "That still doesn't explain the women and the children. Why?"

Nahash put his knife away and started to laugh. "Who do you think I am, governor? What are you trying to do, appeal to my sense of honor and decency? Not only do I like to do things the easy way, but I also deal in the currency of fear. Fear is what makes the world go round, my friend. I want your people to fear me, and to remember me as long as they live."

Nahash paused, and smiled again. "That, and I do also like the eye patch look."

At the end of the conversation Nahash allowed the town to send for help. He'd rather wait seven days to humiliate all of Israel as to wipe out one town now.

The news spread quickly throughout all of Israel. Nahash had been a problem already in the lands of Gad and Rueben, but there was never any talk of eyes being gouged out. The renegade king had gone too far everyone agreed. Something needed to be done. People wept and cried for the sons and daughters of their fellow countrymen.

But other than that, no one did anything.

Though a king, Saul hadn't learned yet that rulers needn't busy themselves with everyday menial things such as physical labor, and was out working on his father's farm. That's when he saw messengers in the town and heard the crying of the people.

"Why is everyone crying?" He asked the messenger as he knocked the mud off his feet.

"Saul, it's because of Jabesh-Gilead. Haven't you heard?"

"No, I'm only the king I suppose," Saul said, recognizing that some changes needed to be made in the royal communication system.

The messenger explained the situation to Saul, and as he spoke it became apparent to Saul that everyone was upset about the situation but no one was actually taking any action to rectify it.

God had touched Saul and made him a different man after his anointing from before. And now the spirit of

God came upon him as he pulled the messenger's sword out from its scabbard.

The people gasped as their new king, in a rage, chopped up two oxen right in front of them. Saul wiped the blood from the blade and gave it back to the messenger.

"Deliver one of these pieces to the leaders of every tribe. You tell them that whoever fails to follow Saul and Samuel will have their oxen wind up like these."

A great fear took hold of the people and they all came together in one consent to go to war against Nahash.

On the morning of the seventh day the new king not only demonstrated that God had touched him, but he also demonstrated that he also had a knack for military strategy. Saul divided the army into three units and they slowly converged upon the Ammonites while they slept.

The morning stillness was shattered as ram's horns signaled the attack order. The men of Israel charged the sleeping mass with sword and spear; many of those on the outskirts of the camp were killed before they had even fully awakened. The others scrambled to their feet, half dressed and groggy, and struggled to gain any resemblance of order. Nahash was screaming orders and kicking men out of their cots.

By the middle of the day the Ammonite army was decimated, no two of them were left together. Nahash had managed to survive and swore his vengeance upon Saul.

The people of Jabesh-Gilead were saved that day because of the zeal of the new king of Israel. Some suggested killing the nay-sayers, but Saul would have none of that.

"There shall not a man be put to death this day," Saul said, "for today the LORD hath wrought salvation in Israel."

Chapter Three

"And the LORD said unto Samuel, Hearken unto the voice of the people in all that they say unto thee: for they have not rejected thee, but they have rejected me, that I should not reign over them."
I Samuel 8:7

1093 B.C. Ramah

The people celebrated their new king and renewed the kingdom in Gilgal. Saul was crowned a second time, as now all the tribes had fully aligned behind him. Sacrifices were offered unto the LORD, and at midday Samuel rose up to speak to the congregation. He reminded them of their sin in asking for a king, when in times past the LORD was their king.

The clouds drew dark, the rain fell, and the people asked for forgiveness for what they had done. But there was no going back, the monarchy was here to stay. Samuel ended the speech with the following words:

"As for me, God forbid I should sin against the LORD in ceasing to pray for thee! I will teach you the good and right way: if ye and your king will do wickedly, then ye both shall be consumed.

"Hearken unto me o Israel: only fear the LORD, and serve him in truth with all your heart: for consider how great things he hath done for you."

* * *

Days later, on an evening like any other, a young man in white walked towards the prophet's house to deliver a message. From behind him a shadowy figure emerged from the darkness.

"So your people have a king now."

Startled and caught off guard, Gabriel drew his sword and turned to face the great accuser. Three darts of fire burst against his sword and the fourth singed his hand causing him to drop the blade.

"Relax," Satan said. "I'm not here to torment you before the time. If I were, you'd already be on your knees before me begging for mercy."

"The time?" Gabriel said cautiously as he picked up his sword.

Satan sighed. "You're as ignorant as your buddy Michael. I will take the earth, I will take Israel, and then I will take Heaven. In the end I will take all the worship of God's creation from him. I may not be able to destroy him, but I will always find. . ." His voice trailed off as Satan smiled and searched for the word. "I will always find a *blessing* in turning his creation against him."

Gabriel was not amused. "The last time you uttered that many 'I wills' you lived to regret it. For what purpose are you here?"

"Just thought I'd have a little fellowship with the Father's favorite little messenger. What do you think about this new turn of events?"

"You mean the monarchy? It's not good; that's what I think," Gabriel said, knowing he wasn't going anywhere for awhile.

"Oh I know! All I have to do is ruin one man and I have the nation! This is absolutely wonderful. You can raise up a thousand prophets, but if I have the king I have the nation."

"They have a good king now," Gabriel replied. "God will keep the nation in good hands."

"Oh come off it, Gabriel!" Satan laughed. "You and I both know that God isn't going to *make* them do anything. That's the biggest flaw in your plan: you're relying on humans to bring in a kingdom on earth. When are you golden boys going to wake up and realize that I won this fight the moment Eve popped that grape into her mouth? They're all fallen and in the end they'll all choose me, and God has it set up so that he has to judge them for doing so."

"The seed will save them."

Satan hissed in fury as he spoke. "The seed is coming from Judah. All I have to do is turn Judah against God so that he'll judge them. It's so easy and predictable."

"Can I go now?"

"No. One thing has been bothering me: why Benjamin? Why is Benjamin on the throne when the scepter is supposed to belong to Judah?"

"Because God is one step ahead of you," Gabriel said. "We're done here."

"Not yet, my friend," Satan said as he placed his hand on the angel. "You had better enjoy your time in the sun while you can. This little toe-hold that you have on my planet will not stand."

Gabriel brushed the hand off his shoulder but Satan continued, spitting the words out with vile contempt. "This kingdom, this kingdom of Israel, will fail. You're so vastly outnumbered. I will break down the hedge. I will corrupt the crown. I will split the kingdom and trample it down to the ground. The prophesies shall fail because there will be no one remaining by whom he can come.

When I'm finished with Israel, God himself shall curse them into obscurity."

Chapter Four

"Therefore thou and thy sons with thee shall keep your
priest's office for every thing of the altar, and within
the vail; and ye shall serve: I have given your priest's
office *unto you* as a service of gift: and the stranger that
cometh nigh shall be put to death."
Numbers 18:7

Not too long after in Gilgal

Saul and his son Jonathan had become heroes in
the land of Israel. It hadn't taken long for Saul
to organize an army and begin attacking the
enemies of Jehovah that had long been plaguing the
people. Jonathan quickly developed the worthy
reputation of a mighty warrior, having smitten a much
larger garrison of Philistine warriors with his own
detachment.

But within this war, more often than not, Israel was
extremely outnumbered and outmatched. While they
fared well against the nomadic Amalekites, the
Philistines were a much greater challenge. The people of
the sea were well trained and had weapons of iron as
opposed to the bronze and copper weapons of the
Hebrews. Much time had passed since the Philistines
had moved south but their efforts to invade Egypt had
failed; now they had returned to Canaan with the intent
of subduing the Hebrews and eventually taking their
territory.

They had done well. While Israel seemed sovereign in her own right, the fact of the matter was that they were under the thumb of the Philistines. And now the Philistines had had enough of the guerrilla attacks upon their armies. This new king and his kingdom had to be stopped.

They formed an army of thirty thousand chariots, six thousand horsemen, and, well, they had lost count of how many thousands of foot-soldiers they had. It was more than enough to put Israel back in its place, and the Hebrews knew it. Fear gripped them to the point that most of the Jewish soldiers were hiding in rocks, caves, thickets and anywhere else they could.

Saul and his loyal troops had frantically withdrawn eastward to Gilgal, attempting to buy time as the massive army of Philistines encamped at Michmash. Though Saul had already proved himself a master tactician, he was clearly out of options. His six hundred men would be massacred if they dared a head-on attack. They were certainly in a tight spot although they weren't exactly pinned, for to the south was the Dead Sea and to the east was the Jordan River. Even if they did attempt to withdraw farther, it left the towns and cities of Israel wide open in the highlands.

He needed help; he had already sent for Samuel the prophet, days ago. He had no other options but to wait for the prophet to arrive with the word of the LORD or wait for the impending doom.

The morning broke as Saul washed his face in a bowl of water. He hadn't slept at all the night before. All night he'd wrestled with the situation he was in, and he knew it was hopeless. He wasn't Gideon or Joshua and this wasn't the battle of Jericho.

Gideon faced an army this size with half as many soldiers as I have, Saul thought as he stared down into the water. *Gideon had God. I'm just a farmboy who happens to be king. I never asked for this job.*

Sadly, when the LORD attempted to impress upon Saul the fact that Gideon was a farmboy as well, one who hadn't asked for the job of delivering Israel, Saul shook it off as his imagination playing games with him.

"Your Majesty?"

Saul looked up to see a scout in front of him. "Yes, son, what do you have for me?"

Out of breath, the young runner huffed the words out between breaths. "Your Majesty, King Saul, the enemy has dispatched raiding parties to the north. They're plundering the highlands."

"What of Michmash and Geba?"

"They're still there."

"Of course they are. They can continue to hold it and threaten us, all the while going after our families and farms."

The commanders had heard the conversation and were growing restless. One of them spoke up now as the scout left. "What are your orders?"

Saul was feeling the same thing, but tried to mask it. "We have no orders as of yet. Samuel will bring us the word of the LORD. He'll offer a sacrifice and then we'll know what to do."

"Your Majesty, they could be on us in a matter of hours. Whatever comfort we have from that report is fleeting."

Saul stood up, his face reddening. "Are you questioning my orders?"

The commander took a step forward and closed the gap between them. "My lord, you haven't given us any orders."

Another commander stood up, attempting to mask his exasperation. "King Saul, time and time again the LORD has delivered our people in times like these. We should attack! The LORD of Hosts shall be our strength!"

Saul spun to face him, his voice now full of bluster as he towered over the smaller man. "I'm in charge here! Don't talk to me about leading a mindless charge and don't attempt to lecture me on our history! Have you forgotten the slaughter of Hormah? When our people valiantly and stupidly charged the Amalekites after the spies' report? There was a reason they wandered in the wilderness for forty years!"

The commander, sufficiently insulted, took a step back and another man took his place. "What would you have us to do then, Saul? Should we fortify here and prepare to defend?"

"No! That's what I'm trying to say, we simply cannot take any action until we hear from Samuel!"

"But Saul, no orders? What am I to tell my men? The morale of the men, sir, they're desperate. If I fail to bring anything back to them we'll have even more deserters!"

That was the last thing Saul needed to hear. He had already lost thousands of soldiers from desertion. He went from being angry to panicking.

"You're right," Saul said. "We simply can't sit here on our hands. We must take action. We have to do something."

"Your Majesty," one of men said compassionately. "You are the LORD's anointed. There's no reason to believe the LORD won't speak to you, especially considering how desperate our situation is."

"I suppose you're right. I'm the leader here, and right now the people need some leadership. I'll offer the sacrifice."

"Are you certain?" the man was startled. "You're a king, not a priest."

"Am I the LORD's anointed, or not? Didn't God tell Joshua to stand upon his feet and take action?"

"Yes, but that was–"

"Stop questioning my authority!" Saul screamed. "You want an order? I'll give you an order! Have your men build me an altar immediately. And somebody get me something to kill."

The day drew on and the men prepared the altar. The sky darkened and it began to rain. Saul's demeanor had completely changed. He was pacing back and forth and muttering to himself. His head turned back and forth frantically, almost as though it twitched.

Hesitantly, a man approached him. "It's ready, my lord."

Saul's eyes bulged as he turned to him. "About time!" Saul stormed over to the animal on the altar and without a second thought slit its throat and lit the fire. He bowed before the altar, prayed and stood back up again.

Right then a raspy voice behind him just about made him jump out of his skin. "Just what do you think you're doing, farmboy?"

Saul spun to face Samuel who was standing directly behind him. The grouchy old prophet looked up at Samuel again and thumped the tip of his bony finger in the king's chest. "Just what exactly do you think you're doing?"

Saul stumbled back, stammering and stuttering. "Samuel! I'm, I'm, I'm so happy you're here!"

Samuel didn't waste time cutting to the chase. "You don't have any business offering that sacrifice, Saul. You broke the law of God. Being a king doesn't put you above the law of the LORD!"

Saul was terrified. "Samuel! No, no, please listen to me! I didn't want to do it, but I had to! I tried to tell them, but they would have left me! The Philistines were coming and so I forced myself to offer it!"

"That's enough! Stop your blubbering, Saul. You've done foolishly: thou hast not kept the commandment of the LORD thy God, which he commanded thee. For now would the LORD have established thy kingdom forever. Thy kingdom shall not continue. He has sought out another.

"The LORD hath sought him a man after his own heart."

Chapter Five

"And his armourbearer said unto him, Do all that *is* in thine heart: turn thee; behold, I *am* with thee according to thy heart."
I Samuel 14:7

The next day near the sharp rocks of Bozez and Seneh

Immediately after having rebuked Saul, Samuel turned and began the five-mile walk to Gibeah. Saul followed, as did the bewildered army of Israel. Upon reaching Gibeah Saul simply sat down under a pomegranate tree and waited. He was pouting, resting, or maybe contemplating his current situation, but for whatever reason no one had the impression that he was praying. The troops, under their own initiative, began establishing some minor defensive fortifications.

The warrior prince, Jonathan, had no interest in taking a seat under a tree or staying on the defense. He stood before his armourbearer with a plan.

"The enemy is up that mountain. I have no intention of simply sitting here idle all the day long. I'm heading up there and I'd like you to come with me. It may be that the LORD will work a great victory for us: for there is no restraint to the LORD to save by many or by few."

The armourbearer understood what that meant. Jonathan was bound and determined to get himself into a fight, and if that meant going solo against a garrison of well-trained soldiers then so be it.

He wasn't going to let that happen. You see, he was an armourbearer, the prince's armourbearer. His jobs were many: one being the maintenance of his master's weaponry. Jonathan was one of the few Hebrews who had iron weapons, having stolen them fair and square from enemies he had slain. Another duty was the transportation of these weapons and armor into battle. Simply put, certain situations called for certain weapons. He also had the task of making sure those whom his master injured never rose again to endanger another Hebrew life.

Most importantly though, a good armourbearer understood his primary job was to give his life for his master. Under no circumstance would he abandon him. He would go where he went; fight whom he fought. Should his master face death, he would die first. Anything else would be unacceptable; anything else would be a disgrace.

"Do all that is in thine heart," the armourbearer said. "Behold, I am with thee according to thine heart."

Jonathan smiled. "I never doubted you, friend. Pack light this time."

The climb was relatively quick and easy as the two of them scrambled up the rocky crag on all fours. Peering over the edge, they spied dozens of enemy warriors milling about.

Ever the optimist, Jonathan said, "Let's let them know we're here. If they come after us, we'll fight here on the side of this mountain. If they do not, we'll go after them."

His companion smiled. "I couldn't help but notice you have no plan where we don't fight them."

Jonathan chuckled and returned the smile. "I suppose the military strategy ends with my father. We'll just have to trust the LORD. Care to do the honors?"

With that the armourbearer peered over the edge and hollered a few uncharitable words at the Philistines. They all laughed and yelled something back about the Hebrew boys coming over there so they could show them a thing or two.

After pulling themselves up, they approached the enemy with swords drawn. Jonathan surmised that there were about fifty soldiers there.

The Philistines didn't even bother to stand. "Are you Hebrew boys lost? Perhaps you're looking for your mothers?" This was followed by laughter and many vile remarks about Jewish women. "Perhaps you're rummaging around looking for your father? You may find his hide decorating the inside of my tent."

"I am fairly certain you do not know my mother," Jonathan said. "But as for my father, you all know him. His name is Saul, and he's the king of this land. That makes you trespassers."

The Hebrews were on them in a flash before they could respond. The prince moved through them swiftly, like a leaf in the shifting wind. The first man slunk to his knees with a diagonal cut to side of his neck. This stopped the blood from reaching his brain, he would bleed out in a couple minutes.

Another man swung at Jonathan, bringing his blade down heavily to the ground. He had missed, and though many soldiers would have sidestepped the attack, Jonathan had slid forward and under it. The back of the man's leg was exposed; the prince pierced the major artery and kept moving.

With Jonathan's technique the enemy was usually slain in a quick and almost bewildering manner. Though efficient it was also anti-climatic, with the encounter ending nearly as quickly as it had begun. The armourbearer lacked his master's grace and typically relied on stunning his foe by bashing him with a shield and then hacking him down.

They went about this for a few minutes and when they finished there were twenty dead Philistines. The remaining enemy soldiers hardened their faces and began to encircle the duo.

Without any warning the ground began to tremble.

* * *

A pomegranate thumped the ground next to Saul and he snapped out of his stupor. He stood up; everywhere around him the world shook. Soldiers stumbled and some fell.

* * *

"LORD, our people need you," the prophet Samuel said. "Saul has failed them. I beseech you to show yourself strong for the host of Israel. Let them know that regardless of their king there is a God in our lands. May the Philistines learn to fear Jehovah this day."

* * *

Jonathan and his armourbearer maintained their balance and watched as the Philistines panicked. The enemy fell upon one another without intent, many were pierced through and others rendered unconscious. God was fighting on behalf of Israel.

* * *

"What's going on here!" Saul barked to his nearest commander.

"I have no idea, sir!" he replied as he steadied himself.

"Are all our troops accounted for? Who is missing?"

"Jonathan and his armourbearer are gone; all others remain, Your Majesty."

* * *

Jonathan and his companion chased after the fleeing Philistines, quickly slaying those that fell from the earthquake. The rocks turned to grass and eventually to woods as they pursued the enemy. Leaning with his back against a tree, Jonathan laughed as his friend breathed heavily with his hands on his knees.

"Did you order that earthquake?" Jonathan said between breaths with a smile.

"I have a feeling Samuel did, my prince."

"Well, will you look at that," Jonathan said, pointing at a branch. Honey was dripping from the tree.

* * *

Saul stood by the priest demanding an answer. "Where is the ark? Where is Samuel? What are we to do?"

The priest held his ground. Ground that was shaking, that is, as they were both struggling to maintain their balance. "I told you before; I do not know where Samuel is! The ark is on its way here now but it will take some time to reach us."

"We must take action now!" Saul snarled. "We don't have time."

"Your Majesty, that is exactly what you said at Gilgal yesterday!" the priest pleaded. "God is placing the same test upon you again! You must wait upon the LORD, the answer is coming!"

Saul cursed and shoved the priest out of his way. "That old man is never here when I need him!" He marched as best as he could to the nearest commander and gave the order: "Attack the enemy now. They are in a state of panic and if we have any chance of saving our kingdom, it's now. I don't want anyone to let up. Give them everything we've got.

Cursed be the man that eateth any thing before I be avenged of mine enemies."

* * *

As Jonathan tasted the honey, his eyes were enlightened. He looked to his armourbearer and said,

"My friend, my father has troubled Israel this day." Something changed within Jonathan at that moment that would forever impact his life. The LORD revealed to him the true nature of his father.

*   *   *

From the rocks and hills they came forth. Out of the caves and dens they sprang. Hebrew warriors were everywhere in the minds of the Philistines. A soldier is useless if he is unable to maintain his balance and at this moment the Philistines were useless. They stumbled and fled, and were slain as they did. That day the children of Israel smote the enemy from Michmash to Aijalon: and the people were very faint.

Later that evening the smell of death hung in the air. Wounded soldiers groaned out for water. They were left to die out on the battlefield, alone.

But they were not alone. Two invisible, though familiar, figures stood on the field of blood and surveyed the carnage.

"Very productive day for the both of us, wouldn't you say?" the darker of the two said.

Michael ignored him and took the life from the crying Philistine.

"That was a very nice earthquake you ordered up there."

"I didn't order anything. Samuel prayed; God ordered and I delivered."

"Why do you have to be so literal about everything, Michael?"

The archangel looked up. "I have no desire to be lifted up with pride."

"Ouch," Satan laughed. "Well, let's just agree that it was a great day for both of us. You delivered your people . . . and I turned the father and son against each other."

"No, you failed. Jonathan will never turn against his father. That young man is impeccable."

Satan sighed. "Well, perhaps you're right. I'll just use his own strength against him if I must. Either way, there were laws broken and vows made recently that I'll not soon forget."

"Saul made that vow; not Jonathan," Michael said, his face hardening.

"Ah, yes he did, didn't he?" Satan smiled. "And that means that as long as Jonathan is loyal to his father, he's subject to that particular vow. He'll either turn on his father or be slain because of his father. I always win in the end, my friend; I always win in the end."

The two parted ways, both attending to their own business.

Chapter Six

"Be sober, be vigilant; because your adversary the
devil, as a roaring lion, walketh about, seeking whom
he may devour:"
I Peter 5:8

1079 B.C. The Land of the Kenites

Many years had passed since the LORD's
initial rejection of Saul as king of Israel.
God in his mercy, however, continued to
allow Saul to reign as king. Saul was a terror to his
enemies as he struggled to establish and spread the
kingdom.

Samuel's prophecy had come true. There was no
mighty man left home, all were conscripted into Saul's
war machine. He battled constantly against the
Philistines, the Ammonites, the Edomites, and the list
went on and on.

There was never peace within the kingdom of Israel
and the constant war brought heaviness to the hearts of
the people. The Israelites who dwelt on the outskirts of
the kingdom, the frontier towns, felt the worst of it as
they were always subject to Amalekite raids. The
innocents were ruthlessly slain and Hebrew women were
taken as the spoils of war. No men of war remained to
protect them; Saul had stolen them all.

As hope became a memory the faith in Jehovah
began to wane for the people and some began to turn to
other devices. Saul had rightly decreed it illegal, but

witchcraft and idol worship began to grow. The kingdom was being strained from within and without.

While the king had never turned to false gods, he had failed to have any passion for the LORD. The man that was once a hero to all became a specter of dread and fear. Oft times he was haunted by evil visions and dreams; at night his men would hear him cry out in his sleep while encamped on the battlefield.

Jonathan, the warrior prince, was disheartened as well. He saw what was happening and knew the LORD was not with the king of Israel. Ever loyal to his father, he never made an attempt at the throne. He had once been a jovial young man filled with a love for the LORD, his father and people; but life was monotonous now and his disposition now matched that of the realm.

Samuel did the best he could with what he had. He gave his all to encourage the people. The embers of patriotism died in the cold night of endless war, but the faithful seer did all he could to keep the nation holding on by faith in Jehovah.

He had delivered yet another message to Saul a week earlier: *The LORD sent me to anoint thee to be king over his people, over Israel: now therefore hearken thou unto the voice of the words of the LORD. Thus saith the LORD of hosts, I remember that which Amalek did to Israel, how he laid wait for him in the way, when he came up from Egypt. Now go and smite Amalek, and utterly destroy all that they have, and spare them not; but slay both man and woman, infant and suckling, ox and sheep, camel and ass.*

The mission was simple and direct: annihilate the Amalekites. Not all that different from the Ammonites, for generations the southern people had plagued Israel and God had had enough. They had brought murder, mayhem, and turmoil to all. And now Saul, for once in a long time, stood ready to honor the word of the LORD.

He had warned the Kenites to flee because he was about to bring the sword of God upon the Amalekite towns. The Kenites dwelt between the Amalekites and the Israelites, but they were cordial to the Hebrews. They were the descendents of Moses' father-in-law Jethro. During the time of the Judges, the great woman Jael was the wife of a Kenite. They had fortified themselves in the rocks and mountains but now fled their country lest they be slain with the enemy.

Saul had amassed an army of over two hundred thousand soldiers. The master tactician had them spread throughout the valley for miles, hidden in rocks and crags of the barren wilderness that made up the home of the Kenite. They had travelled slowly through the wasteland at night to conceal their movements, following advance scouts who also served to warn the indigenous people.

Saul was bold, and having the full assurance that God was behind him he ordered an all-out attack. The armies of God flowed out of the valley and into the land of the Amalekites.

They slew without mercy and regret. Many of the men who attacked had lost their own wives and children to Amalekite raiding parties and were content to return the LORD's vengeance.

That morning had been bright and hot, but as the day wore on the ground became soaked with blood. The skies turned dark and it began to rain. To the world unseen by human eyes the prince of the power of the air had arrived. Michael saw him descend from the skies as darkness swirled about him like a desert sandstorm.

"For what reason are you here, Satan?" Michael asked as the fifth cherub lighted down in front of him and a squad of angels.

"I'd rather not go through it all with you at this time; I simply seek an audience with his Majesty King Saul."

"The LORD hath spoken; thou shalt not interfere with this battle. You understand your orders, you have no leeway here."

Satan smiled. "Michael, Michael, Michael. When will you ever learn the blessedness of the shades of gray? The LORD commanded me not to interfere with the battle itself, which is why your hallowed people have encountered no resistance."

"Leave, Satan. Be gone."

"Nope, not this time. You and I both know the rules. If he submits to God and resists me, then I'll leave. Until then, I have every right to walk by his side."

Michael reached for his sword. "As caretaker of this people I will . . ."

In a blast of darkness Satan had him by the throat and held him off the ground. Michael dropped the sword as the wicked one tightened his grip and hissed the words: "It is you that are stepping outside of your liberties, old friend, and therefore you and your pretty band of angels have no power over me. How far would you wish to take this?"

Michael knew that for once Satan wasn't lying. He relented, and Satan continued on, passing through the midst of the angels as they parted. Walking by Saul the remainder of the day, the deceiver spoke great words of praise to the man. For years Saul had been beaten down and discouraged. The endless wars had their effect on him as well. But today's glory of battle and bloodshed swelled within him, and it stayed within him. He failed to give the glory to Jehovah and the cancerous effects of a prideful heart wore down his will to obey.

All through the day Michael saw it transpire, and it tore him up on the inside. Michael loved the warrior king; he watched the leader come from humble farmboy beginnings to unify the people and threaten all the heathen nations, much like Joshua had. Early on Michael wondered if Saul would be the man that God would use to destroy the enemy nations and claim the ground promised to Abraham nearly a thousand years ago. If the ground was taken perhaps the seed would come and this would all be over.

But as a lamb to the slaughter, Saul was no match for Satan, and Michael was helpless to stop it. Unless Saul prayed for deliverance, no help would come. The tempter puffed him up all day and there would be no request for assistance. The sad thing about pride is that it puts a man in a place where he doesn't believe he needs help. Saul trembled not for the Prince of Darkness grim, because he didn't even know he was there.

And then the moment came. Through the bloodshed and glorious battle around him a messenger ran up to

Saul. "Your Majesty! We have him! We've captured Agag, king of all Amalek. They're bringing him here."

Michael the archangel screamed at Saul. "Kill him! God said to spare not! You must slay utterly! Cursed be he that keepeth back his sword from blood!"

Satan responded by holding up his hand to gain the attention of the angel band. He smiled, waltzed a couple steps towards Saul, and took a bow. Turning towards the king he laughed and drove the spiritual dart deep within his heart. "May the glory be thine, son of Kish, here is your trophy."

Saul thought this was his moment of glory, but instead it was his last chance. He disobeyed the LORD and spared the king and many of the animals.

He had sealed his fate.

Chapter Seven

"And Samuel said, Hath the LORD *as great* delight in burnt offerings and sacrifices, as in obeying the voice of the LORD? Behold, to obey *is* better than sacrifice, *and* to hearken than the fat of rams."
I Samuel 15:22

The next morning in Gilgal

All night long the prophet had prayed. He had no desire to sleep. He wept sore; his eyes were a fountain of tears for the king of Israel. The young man who had become the great hope and pride of the kingdom, he who stood head and shoulders above all and had led thousands into battle time and time again, had fallen.

And it was Samuel's job to deliver the message. God said that he had repented himself from having chosen Saul to be king. Samuel begged for more mercy all night long. With a broken heart the old prophet of God had offered intercessory prayers for the backslidden man.

But that was last night, and now he stood in the middle of the road, blocking the procession of soldiers with Saul in the lead.

The horses neighed as sand swept across the horizon and the king recognized the dreaded silhouette of the preacher. Drawing near, Saul swallowed hard and tasted the dust in the air. He dismounted his horse and spoke rather nervously. "Hello there, Samuel! What a pleasant surprise! I . . ."

Samuel interrupted him. "Did you obey the command of the LORD, Saul?"

"Why, absolutely I did! Why, thou blessed of the LORD, I have performed the commandment of the LORD to the very . . ."

"Then what's that noise over there?"

"That what? Huh?"

Samuel pointed past the heavily-perspiring king. "Why do I hear sheep bleating?"

"Did you say bleeping?"

"No, Saul! I said I hear sheep bleating! Now what sort of mischief are you up to this time, farmboy?"

"Okay, Samuel, listen to me," Saul struggled to say. "The people, they spared the best of the sheep and the oxen to sacrifice. It's not like they weren't going to kill them. They were just going to do it later. They're going to sacrifice them to the LORD. The rest they've already destroyed."

"That's an interesting switch to the third-person plural there, Saul."

"What?"

"Listen," Samuel said. "Do you remember, Saul, when you were little in your own sight? When you were but a young man, reluctant to take the throne? Do you remember when you feared God more than man, Saul?

"The LORD God Jehovah took you from the smallest tribe in Israel and exalted you, Saul, above all others. He chose you and ordained you to finish what Joshua started and utterly destroy the Amalekites.

"And now you speak to me of dawdling and delayed obedience, which is nothing more than disobedience. And you have spared the life of Agag, their king."

In those moments Samuel had become a specter of terror to all that stood nearby. He drove his bony finger into Saul's chest and continued. "God isn't interested in your sacrifice, Saul! He's interested in your obedience. For rebellion is as the sin of witchcraft, and stubbornness is as iniquity and idolatry! Because thou hast rejected the word of the LORD, he hath also rejected thee from being king."

Saul fell to his knees, sniveling. "No, Samuel! I'm sorry, I feared the people! You're right, I sinned! I transgressed the command of the LORD. Please pardon my sin, Samuel! Please forgive me . . . turn again with me that I may worship the LORD . . ."

"I can't pardon you, and you don't need me to worship the LORD! Get up, Saul! I'm not returning with you. You've rejected the word of the LORD, and He's rejected you from being king."

And as Samuel turned to walk away, the desperate Benjamite grasped after him and snagged the prophet's robe. Part of it tore off, and Samuel mercilessly spun again to Saul. "The LORD hath rent the kingdom of Israel from thee this day, and hath given it to a neighbor of thine, that is better than thou. And also the Strength of Israel will not lie nor repent: for he is not a man, that he should repent."

Saul lay there with his face in the dust. Years and years of selfishness, rebellion and hypocrisy were manifesting themselves. He raised a trembling hand.

"Please, don't go. Please stay, please honor me now before the elders of the people, before all Israel. Turn again with me, that I may worship the LORD thy God."

The same compassion and heartache that kept him awake all night came rolling back into Samuel's heart. "Okay, Saul. But this is the last time."

Samuel turned and faced some of the soldiers that stood nearby. "Bring Agag over here."

Quivering and shaking the Amalekite king drew near. His feet shuffled along, bound in chains. He smiled sickly. "Surely the bitterness of death is past?"

Samuel snatched the sword from one of the soldiers before he could react. "As thy sword hath made women childless, so also shall thy mother be childless!"

With a power not his own, Samuel swung the sword at the heathen king removing his hands at the wrists. The king screamed and turned to run but Samuel hacked and chopped at him like a woodsman does a tree. A bloody mess now, the preacher returned the sword to the soldier. "Young man, cursed be he that doeth the work of the LORD deceitfully, and cursed be he that keepeth back his sword from blood."

Time wore on. Instead of the up and downs of the previous years, there were only downs. The Philistine yoke upon the Hebrews grew heavier and heavier. Saul marched troops madly against his enemies on every side, never seeing any measurable level of success.

But for the mercy of Jehovah the kingdom would have been consumed. Though few saw it, the LORD remained and protected his people. His promises remained sure in spite of the weakness and depravity of the king.

And on the day that Samuel rebuked the king, the day in which God's mercy for Saul was ended, the disillusioned soldiers of Israel had stopped believing. Their fearsome warrior king had become a failure, a disgrace, a cursed man and a pathetic excuse for a leader. They, like the entire nation of Israel, had lost all hope.

Little did they know that at that time the light of Israel was just a boy playing with his older brothers in the little town of Bethlehem.

Chapter Eight

"What man of you, having an hundred sheep, if he lose one of them, doth not leave the ninety and nine in the wilderness, and go after that which is lost, until he find it?"
Luke 15:4

1064 B.C. Near Bethlehem

The sounds of a psaltery drifted with the breeze as the tall grass swayed on the sunny hills outside of Bethlehem. The young man sang softly to himself, all the while the sheep bleated and mindlessly chewed grass.

David finished his song, and spoke to the nearest sheep. "My human best, filled with the spirit of God? What did you think?"

The sheep yawned.

The shepherd boy chuckled and half-heartedly tossed a stone at it, smacking it in the rear. It yelped and jumped forward a few steps. David reclined his head on the leather supply pack he brought with him and closed his eyes for a moment, taking in the warmth of the sun. He was thankful for the life he had, thankful for his family, thankful to be a Hebrew and know the true God. His heart was never short on gratitude and humility, and many times like this the Holy Spirit of Jehovah would fill the heart of the young man with songs of praise out alone on the hills of Judea.

David shivered as he felt a cool breeze come from the west. He heard the subtle cry of a ewe lamb and looked up just in time to see the hind end and flickering tail of a lion disappearing into the nearby woods. The dark and chill breeze came again, crawling up his neck and whispered to his ear, *Leave it. It's only one lamb, no point in dying over only one.*

David snapped his eyes shut and shook his head. This wasn't the first time the darkness had spoken to him, especially after times of praise such as this one. The same heart that overflowed with emotion for the LORD seemed to be a prime target for the wicked one. It was almost as if his greatest strength was his corresponding weakness.

But regardless of his feelings, this was a good shepherd and he was no hireling. *It's never only one lamb,* he thought as he scooped up the bag of stones. *The beast will return again and again, seeking whom it may devour.*

A few steps into pursuing the lion David was stopped by another noise behind him. David didn't look back; he just stood still and listened. He recognized that sound. It wasn't loud or overbearing, nor was it shrill or sharp. It was the sound of leaves crackling mixed with the heavy breathing of a bear.

This can't be possible, David thought.

Without a second thought he turned and faced the bear. It was on the other side of the flock, lumbering forward on all fours in no apparent hurry. David dropped a rock in the sling and sprinted towards the bear. On the third rotation he released the rock and it thumped against the beast's shoulder.

The bear stood on his back feet and let out a roar. The senseless sheep were finally awakened to the situation and began to scatter. The beast, unphased but now enraged, stood swiping at the air and roaring.

Most normal people would have turned and run or perhaps look for a tree, but David released another rock and it hit the bear in the throat. The bear, on all fours now, coughed and hacked.

Still running towards it, David closed the gap between himself and the bear. His hand found the shepherd's staff on the ground; he scooped it up as he came within reach of the animal. The bear roared and David shoved the staff in its mouth as deep as he could.

The bear fell forward and the rod snapped. The beast struggled, grasping at its mouth, desperately trying to remove the wood that had pierced its throat and belly. For David, there was no hesitation; there was no drawing back or second guessing. While the bear wallowed in its bloody misery, David placed the largest rock he had in his sling and swung it as hard as he could. There was no need to release the rock; with it still in the sling he struck the bear in the skull enough times to ensure its death.

He took a breath. Quickly now, David placed his fingers to his mouth and made the shrill whistle that his sheep heard and heeded. They ran towards him, bleating and confused. He tried to calm them down. Then he remembered the one missing lamb.

It's dead and gone by now, the darkness said. *There's no point in going after it.*

Crashing through the undergrowth, David's eyes darted ahead desperately searching for any sign. He jumped a log and ducked under a branch, and ran through a shallow stream. He knew that if the lamb was alive it would only be by the sheer mercies of God.

Looking up, he saw it: by the gentle flowing stream the lion was lazily lying down with lamb. David expected it to be tearing into it with his fangs, but it just sat there with its enormous paw on the frightened animal, holding it in place. Supernatural forces were at work, and another voice spoke to David's heart now. *In due season we shall reap, if we faint not.* The lion grabbed the lamb by the scruff of its neck and stood up.

It turned its head and looked at David, with the lamb dangling from its maw, as if to mock him. David charged it as before, and the stone flew through the air hitting animal in the side of the ribcage. The impact knocked the wind out of the beast and David snatched the lamb from its mouth and tossed it to the side where it would be safe.

The lion slapped at David with its paw, knocking him to the side and leaving three gashes in his chest. The pain was terrible. It left him gagging and in shock. He had taken one hit from the lion, and David was certain a rib or two had cracked. If he didn't return home soon, he'd bleed to death. This would be over quickly, one way or another.

The lion sprung, and desperately trying to ignore his pain David rolled to the side. It reached for him, as a cat would a mouse, with its paw striking the ground within inches of him. David pulled a dagger from his belt and cut its paw. The lion lifted its head and roared in pain, and as it did, David grabbed its beard with one hand and plunged the knife into its throat with the other.

David, lying on his back now, covered his face and wept.

The Angel of the LORD stood by, and next to him was Satan. The LORD looked to him and spoke, "That is the man after my own heart."

Chapter Nine

"Thou tellest my wanderings: put thou my tears into thy bottle: *are they* not in thy book?"
Psalm 56:8

1063 B.C. Ramah

If there was ever a man of sorrows who was acquainted with grief, it was Samuel. As a child he had the shock of being left by his mother to spend his life working in the temple. He followed the LORD and was rejected by the vile Hophni and Phinehas, the only friend and role model in his life being Eli the priest. Then the terrible day came in which he was commanded by God to bring a message of condemnation to Eli. He was also there the day the glory departed from Israel and the ark was taken - the day Eli and his sons had died.

Samuel saw his own sons turn away from the right way, just as Eli's boys had done. He had now seen the demise of Saul and knew the worst was yet to come.

It was just another day for the old man as he knelt beside his bed. Though familiar, he was never able to grow accustom to the old feeling of sadness. Just as the LORD had interrupted another man in the middle of despondent prayer a several hundred years ago, Samuel was about to be interrupted in prayer right now.

"How long wilt thou mourn for Saul, seeing I have rejected him from reigning over Israel? Fill thine horn with oil, and go, I will send thee to Jesse the

Bethlehemite: for I have provided me a king among his sons."

The time for treason against the king had come. He was the first to stand for Saul, and now he had to be the first to stand against him. Such was the role of a prophet, especially one like Samuel.

"LORD, how can I go? If Saul hears it, he'll kill me."

"Take an heifer with you and say that you are come to sacrifice unto the LORD. Call Jesse to the sacrifice, and thou shalt anoint unto me him whom I name unto thee."

* * *

The LORD of creation sat upon his throne, with the host of Heaven at his right hand and his left. "Who shall trouble Saul, king of Israel, that he may seek out the son of Jesse to play the harp for him?"

* * *

At Bethlehem, the elders were troubled at the arrival of Samuel, but they knew better than to try and stop him. Anyone with any sense knew he had ulterior motives than simply offering a sacrifice. Satisfied with the excuse, the elders conspired to stay out of the way. After all, everyone would love to see Saul go.

Following the sacrifice, Samuel went to Jesse's house. It was like any other Israelite stone house, rectangle in shape with a staircase leading to a flat roof. Inside the house Samuel explained the situation to Jesse, and Jesse called seven of his sons before Samuel.

Samuel smiled as he looked at the young men. "You must be proud, Jesse. This is a fine group of boys you have here. I believe the next king of Israel is going to be one of these boys."

Samuel looked to the young men and spoke again. "Now I'm going to pray and the LORD is going to show me which one of you is to be king. I'm an old and tired man so when I call you, you come over here and let me get a good look at you."

The boys smiled at each other and at the prophet. They still hadn't decided if he was crazy or intentionally playing games with them, but he was Samuel and if anyone had the right to be crazy it was he.

The first to pass before Samuel was the oldest, Eliab. Already in the army, he was tall, strong and fit. The people would have no problem in following a man of this stature. *This has to be the one,* Samuel thought. *A warrior just like Saul.*

The LORD interrupted his thoughts. *I'm looking for a warrior all right, but it's not the one you're thinking. Look not on his countenance, or on the height of his stature; because I have refused him: for the LORD seeth not as man seeth; for man looketh on the outward appearance, but the LORD looketh on the heart."*

Samuel spoke to Jesse. "That's not the one."

They all passed before him, and not one of them was selected. "Any others, Jesse?"

* * *

The evil spirit circled high above the throne of Israel, eager to inflame and provoke King Saul. The Holy Spirit stood by as his protector, but soon the hedge would fall.

* * *

"There's another, the youngest. He's out watching the sheep. I didn't honestly think it would come down to him."

"Did you say he's a shepherd?" Samuel said.

"That's right."

Samuel smiled. "Tell him to come, and hurry. No one sit down until I see this young shepherd."

Minutes later David entered the room. He was a fine looking young man with reddish skin and auburn hair. He wasn't spectacular or imposing in his physical features, though he was certainly masculine and his countenance displayed an aura of confidence. He carried himself like a man with a clear conscience, his gaze never glancing away or hesitating. Those eyes feared no man or beast. They only feared the LORD.

The LORD spoke immediately to Samuel, *Arise and anoint him: for this is he.* As he knelt before the prophet, the oil flowed over his head, and within the halls of Heaven angels sounded the coronation music.

The Holy Spirit left Saul and the evil spirit took his place.

The oil ran down the back of David's head and he watched as it dripped onto the floor. As he felt the oil on his skin, he also felt the anointing of the Holy Spirit upon him. He had felt the LORD's presence before, but this was something entirely different and David loved it. He knew he needed it and never wanted it to be taken from him. David wasn't excited about being king; he was excited about being closer to the LORD.

As the prophet placed his hands upon him and prayed, David quietly breathed the words, "As the hart panteth after the water brooks, so panteth my soul after thee, O God."

Chapter Ten

"And the king said, Enquire thou whose son the stripling *is.*"
I Samuel 17:56

Later that year by the Valley of Elah

The days passed and David continued to do what he always did. Throughout his childhood he had become very knowledgeable of terrain and survival. He lived out on the hills of Judea tending to his sheep. He continued to grow as a warrior and psalmist and lived off of a diet of olives, cheese and bread.

The see-saw war between Israel and the Philistines had endured. Saul, living in Gibeah not more than seven miles away from David, had become oppressed by a demonic spirit and suffered fits of madness. A temporary solution had been found in music. David had not only become the musician to drive away Saul's demon, but he had also become one of Saul's many armourbearers. David's life was extremely encumbered between taking care of sheep for his father and driving away demons for the king.

Though today seemed like any other day for the young man, it would be the defining moment of his life. For many people that moment comes late in life, or when one is more established, but not for David. For David, the greatest moment, or at least the most legendary moment of his life, was to occur when he was young, innocent, and little in his own sight.

* * *

Jonathan slammed his fist down on the wooden table, shaking everything on it. "He's mine, I can kill him! Just let me, Father."

Saul felt the back of his neck with his hand and just stared down. In front of him were maps and objects used to devise troop formations. The war room was mostly dark, lit only by the light that streamed in from the tent door.

"Son, I can't–"

Jonathan heaved a roar of disgust and with one swoop of his arm he shoved everything off the table. "May your schemes and cowardice return to the pit from whence they came! Father, if you won't face this uncircumcised monster of Gath than at least allow me to!"

"That's enough!" Saul said as he put a finger to Jonathan's face. "We will have decorum here and though you are my son, I am still your king. It is reckless and foolish for either one of us to fight this man alone. We would never do so on the battlefield and it is stupid to even consider it under these circumstances."

Jonathan had regained his composure by now. "Forgive me, Father, but what else are we supposed to do?"

"We wait for a volunteer," Saul said. "Some men are so desperate they'll do anything."

* * *

The three eldest sons of Jessie sat on the grassy hillside. All around them the armies of Israel did the same, all the while gazing off into the Valley of Elah and the Philistine-infested hill on the other side. "Here comes the little king now," Eliab said as he elbowed Shammah.

The younger brother looked over his shoulder to see David calling their names and carrying a bag of food. "Thank God he's finally here. I'm starving."

When David reached them he was eager to hear the news of the battle. "Why is there no fighting? Have they surrendered? How goes the battle?"

Eliab just bit into his bread and grunted.

"What?" David said. "Why does everyone here look so sad and. . . grouchy?"

"That's why," Shammah said as he nodded in the direction of the valley.

And there he was, his feet pounding the ground as he raised his spear to the skies, Goliath of Gath.

* * *

"Whoever we send out there is a dead man. We all know that," Saul said to his commanding officers.

This is all so very inspiring, Jonathan thought.

"We have to prepare for defeat, men. It's a matter of mitigating the loss in morale that the army will certainly endure. Either they have to be able to fight demoralized or we have to find a way to escape this scenario and fight another day."

One of the more brazen commanders stepped forward. "Your Majesty, forgive me, but I can't believe you are saying this. These are valiant men we have here. How exactly are they supposed to plan to fail? Are we to send some miserable dunce out to fight and the rest of us simply run away? Could you please tell us what you are suggesting here?"

"What I am suggesting, Commander, is that we find a way to survive in spite of our circumstances."

* * *

Both hills grew silent as the mammoth of a man swaggered out into the middle of the valley. He was nearly ten feet tall and his armor consisted of scales of polished brass; heavy, large and thick, which was virtually impenetrable weighing over two-hundred pounds. Goliath was not merely a large and lumbering Anakim, he was a leader and champion of his people. He understood the confusion of the battlefield and was armored everywhere, including his back. The Philistine carried a spear that matched his height and was nearly three inches round, occasionally mistaken as a small tree; the spearhead itself weighed fifteen pounds. Content to usually smash his opponents to death with his spear, he rarely drew his sword. That sword, however, was about four feet long and rested in a leather scabbard strapped to his back.

The giant's voice was loud and clear as he shouted. He mocked and blasphemed the Hebrew God and the armies of Israel. He spoke of taking the soldier's wives and daughters to his tent and killing their sons. He laughed and applauded the deafening silence after barking the challenge: "Send me a man that we may fight!"

David spoke to his brothers. "This pagan has brought a reproach to the name of our God! Who's going to fight him? Who does this uncircumcised Philistine think he is talking like that about our God and our people?"

A soldier in the same area answered. "There's been no volunteers yet, boy! But whoever it is that takes him on, providing I suppose that he survives and all, will win the hand of the king's daughter and great riches. Also, his father's house will be free in Israel, no taxes, no conscription – free I say, free!"

David was about to answer but Eliab put his hand up. "Be quiet David! I know how you are and what's in your heart. You're here to see the battle and cause problems! Go back home now!"

"What did I do that was so wrong?" David answered. "And why haven't we had a volunteer yet? What is wrong with our people? We should be fighting each other for a chance to go out there and kill that filthy pagan! You hear what he said about our God?

"Where is the courage? Where are the men of valour? Have we forgotten who we are? Have we forgotten who our God is? Is there not a cause?"

* * *

"Father," Jonathan said, "may I have a word with you in private?"

"Certainly, son," Saul replied as his commanders left the room.

"I apologize for being so forward with you; I know and understand my position. Please hear me out though: should you or I die in battle the army will be enraged. They'll fight like a bear bereaved of her whelps. You send anyone else and they'll see themselves as fallen and weak should he fail. I'm willing to die in that valley, father. If you won't go, then send me."

"Son, you won't be dying today. The kingdom will be yours one day."

Jonathan was frustrated. "Why? Why were you so eager to save your skin and have me slain at Michmash, but now my life is—"

Just then a man poked his head into the tent. "Your Majesty, we have a volunteer." The man explained what David had said, and Saul asked to see him.

David walked into the tent, took a knee and bowed his head. "Let no man's heart fail because of him; thy servant will go and fight with this Philistine."

Jonathan grabbed his father. "Don't. Please."

Saul gave him one last look, and turned to speak to the boy.

* * *

"Why are you scooping up four other stones, David? You're not going to have time to get them off." Eliab said, standing beside his younger brother.

"In case his sons come out after him."

"Don't you mean his brothers? Look, you're a dead man if you head out there. You don't stand a chance."

David sighed and put the stones in the pouch on his hip. The two of them walked silently towards the Valley of Elah. Eliab wasn't really all that fond of David, but David was still his younger brother and he still loved him. His mind raced for something to say. He also wondered what to tell Jesse when he brought the boy home in pieces.

David stopped at the edge of the valley and turned to face Eliab. "If Samuel was right and I'm to be king then I won't die. God isn't finished with me yet."

"Samuel is old," Eliab said emphatically, his eyes glancing towards the silhouette of the giant behind David. "How do you know he wasn't being senile?"

David cracked a smile. "Samuel's always been old. I guess now we'll find out if he's senile too."

Minutes later David was alone in the valley with Goliath and the giant's armourbearer who held a shield in front of the Philistine. David didn't attempt to bring anything new into the battle, all he had was his staff and the pouch on his hip that contained five stones. The two of them stood there looking at each other until Goliath held his hand up to block the sun from his view.

"Is that a little shepherd boy?" He roared, laughing, his voice clearly heard by both armies. "Is that a shepherd boy or one of Saul's daughters? I asked for a man, not a princess. Am I supposed to kill it or take it home to slop my pigs?

"Is this the greatest warrior you can bring me? Am I a dog, that thou comest to me with staves? Is he here to slay me with that staff?"

As the Philistine continued to roar and curse David by his gods, the boy's mind went to what Jonathan had said to him. *The world has yet to see what God can do with a man fully consecrated to him.*

David drew closer, but Goliath wouldn't shut up. "That's right, come here young one. I'll skin you alive, boy. Come to me, and I will give thy flesh unto the fowls of the air, and to the beasts of the field."

David held his staff high in the air, and pointed the end directly at the giant. "Thou comest to me with a sword, and with a spear, and with a shield: but I come to thee in the name of the LORD of hosts, the God of the armies of Israel, whom thou hast defied.

"This day will the LORD deliver thee into mine hand; and I will smite thee, and take thine head from thee; and I will give the carcases of the host of the Philistines this day unto the fowls of the air, and to the wild beasts of the earth; that all the earth may know that there is a God in Israel.

"And all this assembly shall know that the LORD saveth not with sword and spear: for the battle is the LORD'S, and he will give you into our hands."

Goliath smiled, and tightened his grip on the massive spear in his right hand. "Let's see if you can fight as well as you can talk."

The beast of a man drew his head back and roared to the heavens. Then he forsook his armourbearer and charged towards the boy, the demon battle-rage coursed through his body as the dirt kicked up behind him. David ran towards the giant as well, staff in hand.

Now within range, Goliath halted and quickly rotated the spear in his hand and heaved it at the young man. David leaned his head and torso to the right, dodging the spear, and never stopped his forward momentum.

Goliath smirked, and reached for the sword on his back. Something caught his eye for a moment and he hesitated. David had dropped his staff and it was now evident that he was also holding a sling. Two words entered the mind of the giant at this point: *my helmet.*

Goliath may have been overconfident, but he wasn't stupid. He was a seasoned warrior and understood the accuracy of Israelite slingers. He knew of the Canaanite invasion and he had seen first hand their potential.

He felt a sudden dip in confidence. Glancing back Goliath saw his armourbearer running towards him, helmet in hand. The giant knew that was foolish now because in one way or another this would be over in a matter of seconds.

When Goliath looked back at the Hebrew, David's arm was outstretched: he had released the stone. It struck him directly in the forehead and his head jerked back. He took one step forward, his eyes glossy and empty, and fell face first into the dust and weeds of the now forever infamous valley of Elam.

David scurried up to the corpse of the giant and placed his foot upon its back. The last bit of air gurgled out of the Philistine as David drew the giant's own sword from his back scabbard. Grabbing the enemy's hair, David jerked the head up and raised the sword high in the air. For a brief moment the glare of the sun reflected off the blade and then it came down, decapitating the giant.

With both hands outstretched, David held the head of the giant in the air before the Israelite army and yelled the words: "Is there not a cause?"

Chapter Eleven

**"Let us go forth therefore unto him without the camp,
bearing his reproach."
Hebrews 13:13**

Three years later in the wilderness of Ziph

Silently the figure moved alone through the woods, the black of night concealing his movements. The man was in his forties; strong, tall and confident, he wasn't the sort to be intimidated or slowed by anyone, and yet his countenance showed a weariness of a man twice his age. Upon his shoulder he wore a red cloak, and his shield bore the crest of the royal house of Saul.

As he made his way through the woods he came upon a couple of sentries. They instantly recognized him and nodded as he passed by and entered the camp. They were renegades, all men on the run because of distress, debt and discontentment. At the cave of Adullam they joined to become a vicious strike force that could move swiftly, living off the land.

As if out of nowhere, a hand grabbed the man from behind on the shoulder and turned him.

"Jonathan, my dear friend," David said as he hugged him. The two sat down across from each other by a fire and one of the men gave them each something to drink.

Jonathan looked around and sighed. "Much can surely happen in a few years, hmm? What's that you're writing?"

David looked over to the side, saw the parchment and handed it to Jonathan.

Jonathan eyed it quickly, reading some of it aloud. "My God, my God, why hast thou forsaken me? They part my garments among them, and cast lots upon my vesture... a seed shall serve him... they shall come, and shall declare his righteousness unto a people that shall be born."

Jonathan looked at David. "What is all this about?"

"I'm not exactly sure, to be honest."

"But you wrote it! And it doesn't make any sense!"

David smiled. "I'm a psalmist; I never said I was a good one. God told me to write it. I think it's about the Daysman."

"Job's Daysman?"

"That's the one, the seed."

Jonathan scratched his beard. "But this talks about a seed being plural, not one man. What's that about?"

David laughed. "As I told you, I'm not exactly sure!"

A moment or two of silence passed between the two of them, and David spoke up again. "How have you been, old friend?"

Jonathan stared into the fire. "Terrible. My father battles constantly against the Philistines and never is there any real victory because there is no real blessing. We've done this for decades, and for decades our frontiers have been ravaged by the Amalekites.

"The last real victory was when you slew that beast from Gath."

Looking past David now, Jonathan saw the great sword. "I see you reacquired the famous sword."

"Yes, the priests gave it to me," David said.

Jonathan's eyes locked onto David's for a moment, and then looked away, filled with guilt.

David sensed it and treaded lightly. "My friend, I still remember that day. You gave me your sword and bow. I was a boy, and you honored me in front of the king and his men. We fought together. We made covenants to protect each other. I'm alive today because of you.

"I know you love your father, but you need to forsake him. He's cursed of God; the blessing has been replaced with a curse."

Jonathan winced. "I can't leave him. He's my father."

"You must. He's tried to kill me repeatedly, and he's even tried to kill you. He's a murderer; the blood of eighty-five priests and the entire city of Nob stain his hands. He slew children in that town, Jonathan!"

"Doeg killed them, not my father."

David just stared at him.

Jonathan looked at the ground. "But my father gave the order."

David spoke again. "Your father is under the influence of unclean spirits. Half of the time he's insane. He's not the man he used to be. You have no business staying under his command. If it were any other man, you would have already deserted.

"I know you see the truth; you're older and wiser than I. You have more courage than any man I know. Why can't you leave?"

Jonathan looked up. "It's not courage."

"I know it's not. It's your loyalty. But you're loyal to the wrong thing. You're loyal to the wrong man, Jonathan. You need to join me here."

Jonathan held up his hand. "I understand, but I can't desert my father. He needs me."

"You'll die by his side," David said.

"Perhaps so. But God placed me under his rule and authority. I am his son, and I will forever be his son," Jonathan continued.

"I know you will be king one day, David. The LORD has anointed thee to this purpose. When you are king you'll have my support. My father refuses to acknowledge this, but he knows it. I'm happy to be second in the kingdom in the kingdom now, and I'll be happy to be then as well."

David arose and clasped Jonathan's hand. "You've made your decision. Farwell, my friend.

"Farwell, Lion of Judah. 'Till that illustrious day shall rise, encourage thyself in the LORD thy God."

Chapter Twelve

"Then said Samuel, Wherefore then dost thou ask of
me, seeing the LORD is departed from thee, and is
become thine enemy?"
I Samuel 28:16

1056 B.C. Endor

Many years had passed from that fateful meeting between Jonathan and David in the woods of Ziph. This was a night that from the surface looked somewhat similar. Three men crept through the woods and in the dark of night to a mysterious destination. They were all dressed in tattered brownish garments; their faces were concealed with hoods.

The tallest man, in the middle of the group, was twitching nervously. He kept turning his head to the left and the right, all the while muttering under his breath.

"Your Majesty," one of the men whispered, "you'll pardon me for saying so, but you may want to be a little quieter."

The mad king's eyes bulged as he responded. "I need to speak to Samuel!"

"He's dead, King. You can't. I'm sorry. This is the best we can do."

Saul continued to talk to himself disjointedly. "The Urim. The Thummim. The breastplate. Curse Abiathar! They've all turned against me! Where's Doeg?"

"Your Majesty! Please speak quietly!" one of the men said.

This went on for a good while until the group came upon a little wooden cottage. It was shrouded by trees and had a spiritual darkness that enveloped it.

"No, I need to speak to a prophet!" Saul said. "Where are the prophets?"

"They're gone. They've all fled."

"The Philistines. There's too many of them. The Urim! The Thummim! David has the breastplate! We'll be slaughtered!"

One of the men leaned over to the other. "Oh goodnight, he's full of them, isn't he?"

"What's that?" Saul said wildly.

"Never mind, my king. Shall we?" the man said as he gestured to the door.

"Very well," Saul said as he raised his hand to knock.

* * *

While Saul dealt with his own struggles, one must briefly consider David and where his journey had led him over the years. David and his mighty men had made an alliance with the Philistines in an attempt to provide a defense for their own families who were now dwelling in the Philistine town of Ziklag.

The Philistine king, Achish, had come to respect David and believed that he had turned on his own people. This, of course, wasn't true. David had given a false report of his actions: he wasn't attacking the south of Judah and the Kenites, he had been fighting the Amalekites and other rovers.

Satan had prepared a trap for David. The Philistines were encamped at Aphek, and David was with them. They were preparing to fight the Hebrews. David was in an impossible situation: fight the Hebrews and never be king of Israel, or turn on the massive Philistine army and die.

*   *   *

The old wooden door creaked upon its hinges; the light from inside the dwelling spilled onto the ground in front of Saul and his men. The door opened and the stench of filth and rottenness was overwhelming as a snaggletooth old woman greeted them.

"Three men outside my door at this hour?" she hacked, "Whadaya want?"

Saul, who was disguised as a common soldier, though a very tall common soldier, was the first to speak. "I want, er, we want to talk to Samuel!"

The old hag cackled and coughed and hacked and snorted and made all sorts of noises that generally made everyone feel uncomfortable. "Why in the world d' you wanna talk to him?"

When no one answered, she spoke again. "My necromancin' days are over, boys. Saul made a law and now me and all my professional associates have had to turn to other lines of work to make ends meet! I'd rather keep my head where it is, thank-you very much."

She started to close the door but Saul grabbed it. "Please, madam. You have nothing to worry about. As the LORD liveth, there shall no punishment come to you for this thing."

"All right, come on in," she said as she turned and left the door open for them.

The three men walked inside, wincing and holding their breath all the while being very careful where they stepped. "Breath through your mouth," one of them grunted to the other. All over the floor there were dead things: dead frogs, dead sheep, dead dogs, dead rabbits, dead—

"We're gonna head down here," the old witch said as she opened up a trap door in the floor. "Grab that torch over there will ya, string-bean?" she said motioning to Saul.

"What's a string-bean?" Saul whispered to the man next to him as they headed down the deep hole. Down, down, down they went where the air became thick and wet and the slime on the walls glistened in the firelight. Finally they reached a little room.

"What is this place?" one of the men asked.

"It's called a basement, genius! It's where young men live until their mothers kick them out. Or, in my case, it's where I perform all my shenanigans."

"I hate that word," Saul said.

"Okay, everyone stand back now!" the old hag said, bending over with her arms outstretched. She started crushing bones and throwing the dust in the air. She grabbed one of her dead things and tore its ribcage open, much to the disgust of everyone around her. Then she sat down cross-legged and started humming.

And she hummed some more. More and more she hummed until something rather amazing happened.

A sudden high-pitched whine was heard. Everyone in the room was blown back by a large hole in the ground that had immediately opened up with a sudden rushing wind, filling the place with light.

"Well that's never happened before," the witch of Endor said as she stood up, dusting herself off. She looked over to Saul, who was staring at the torrent of light coming from the hole in the ground, and finally recognized him as Saul. "You're Saul! Why'd you lie to me?"

"Don't be afraid," Saul said. "What did you see in there?"

The old woman crept forward and leaned over the hole, peering down into the deep abyss. The wind blew her mangy gray hair back as she yelled to the other men. "It's him all right, Samuel is coming up! And there's a couple of those gods coming up with him!"

"Other gods?" one of the men said to the other.

"Sons of God. Usually not a good thing."

Without any prior indication all the noise and wind and light suddenly stopped. And before them stood the old prayer warrior, the last judge of Israel, the great seer of seers: Samuel the prophet of Israel.

"Why hast thou disquieted me, to bring me up? I was at rest, at peace, waiting with the others for the Messiah to come," Samuel said.

Saul was stooping before the soul of the man that had anointed him king so many years ago. How much sadder and more tragic was this scene was than that one. A young and humble man with his entire life and the hope of all Israel behind him, versus the shattered and vacillating tyrant who had the blood of innocents on his hands and the curse of God on his head.

"God won't listen to me, Samuel. I don't have the breastplate. No prophets, no dreams, nothing. I'm afraid, Samuel. The Philistines— there's so many of them. I've called for you because I don't know what to do! What should I do, Samuel! What do I do?"

The voice of the seer was strong, and unhesitant. "How can I help you, Saul? If God is your enemy, then how can I help you?"

Saul tried to speak, but Samuel wouldn't let up.

"The LORD has rent out of thine hand the kingdom, and given it to thy neighbor. It's David's kingdom. It's been his kingdom since the day I anointed him, Saul. It's his kingdom whether he's sitting on the throne or not.

"Because thou obeyest not the voice of the LORD, nor executed his fierce wrath upon Amalek, therefore the LORD hast done this thing upon thee this day.

"Tomorrow, you and your sons out on the battlefield, will die. You'll be with me. The end has come for you, Saul.

"The LORD will deliver the host of Israel unto the Philistines tomorrow."

Chapter Thirteen

"From the blood of the slain, from the fat of the mighty, the bow of Jonathan turned not back, and the sword of Saul returned not empty."
II Samuel 1:22

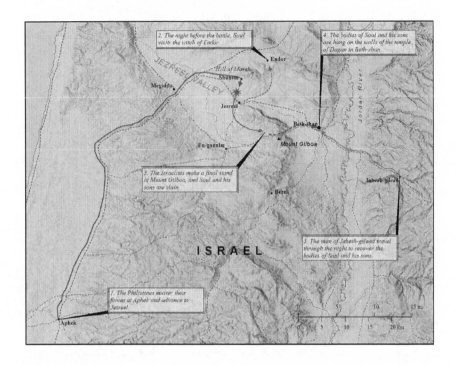

The Next Day: Mount Gilboa

Saul and Jonathan stood atop the mount and looked into the fertile plains of Jezreel. Before them was the largest enemy force that Saul had ever faced: the valley was filled with a mass of archers, swordsmen and spearmen, cavalrymen and charioteers. For years and years Saul had kept the more advanced

Philistine nation off guard by fighting them where he wanted to fight and how he wanted to fight.

That strategy had never changed. The force assembled was much too powerful for an all-out assault, and so Saul and his men had stayed to the ridges and mountains as best they could. The Philistines, hindered by their chariots, had progressively moved through the valleys and passes all the while garnering additional support from Canaanite mercenaries. They had also gathered what seemed to be every last Philistine soldier they could from every town on the way.

Saul turned to his son. "The lords of the Philistines are all here. Guaranteed they've left many of their cities undefended. It's a pity we're here."

Jonathan examined the purple iris flower in his hand. "What do you mean?"

"Go. Rally the forces in Dan. You're the only man who can do it. Hit the sea filth at their homes while their guard is down."

"I'm not going to leave you, Father. I'm not going to forsake you at this time."

"My time has come, son."

"You don't know that, Father. I seem to remember a farmer who wiped out the Midianites in this valley a couple hundred years ago."

Saul looked at his son and smiled. *"Maybe so,"* he thought, *"but last night's fleece didn't give good news."*

*   *   *

A few days before that conversation had occurred the Philistine king was speaking with the commander of his greatest mercenary force. "I'm sorry David," Achish said, "but the lords don't trust you."

"Why? In what way have I failed you?" David insisted, "I've done everything you've asked and abhorred myself of Saul's kingdom. What have I done that would prevent me from fighting against the enemies of my lord the king?"

"David, they remember Michmash and Gibeah. Saul had only six-hundred troops and we could have crushed him. There was an earthquake, and our Hebrew mercenaries betrayed us that day and changed everything. The Hebrews that turned on us were welcomed back to the ranks of Israel."

So much for that idea, David thought.

Achish continued, "You've been ordered to return to Ziklag."

* * *

The fighting had begun. The ridges of Mount Gilboa branched off from the Samarian Mountains heading north to northwest for nearly twelve miles. Saul's forces held the rocky heights while the enemy struggled upwards.

On all sides Jewish swordsmen had met them near the bottom of the hills and gradually withdrawn up towards the top. The enemy continued to slam against them on the ridge, pushing them ever backwards.

Hebrew archers and slingers supported them from the top.

Saul and his three sons were at the southwestern foothills when a runner came to him.

"The main attack is in the center, my lord. Do you have any further orders?"

Jonathan drew the bowstring to his mouth and let an arrow fly. It struck a Philistine that was warily making the treacherous hike towards them. Jonathan interrupted Saul before he could speak to the runner. "Father, we can hold them all day."

"Son, we'll *have* to hold them all day; they're just too many of them."

As Saul turned to speak to the runner something caught his eye. Holding his hand up to block the sun he saw it: a large mass of chariots leaving the main group and heading west, far from the Gilboa ridge and away from the battlefield. Saul sighed within himself and spoke to the runner. "What of Gina? Do they stand prepared?"

The runner was confident. "They do indeed, Your Majesty."

Saul cursed for doubt. "Move any reserve troops to the south of the ridge, bring them here."

"Leave the center? That's where the main assault is."

"Those are my orders."

* * *

The horse hooves kicked up dirt and grass behind them as the chariots tore across the grassy plain at full speed. Other than their seeming monopoly of iron, the chariot was Philistia's greatest strength. Fast and maneuverable, the archer chariot was so powerful as a support unit that the Philistines never bothered to use archers on foot.

The men of Gina held their ground as the enemy drew nigh.

* * *

"Pull our reserves?" the commander yelled to the runner. The noise of the battle had reached a fever pitch; the Philistines were pushing their way up the mountain and the men of Israel were falling before them.

"That's what the king said," the runner said, gasping for breath.

"Tell the king we don't have any reserves! They keep breaking through!"

The runner looked at the scene before him. On the edge of the mountain the Israelite artillery were hurling arrows and rocks to the endless horde of Philistine warriors. The enemy filled the mount like a swarm of angry ants. Over and over again they would break through the Israelite line, and then the Hebrews would fall back and reform only to break again.

The commander continued. "We need water. Tell the king my men are parched. They can't fight if they can't stand."

* * *

The lead chariot came to a halt before the group of soldiers. The commander walked forward with three other soldiers behind him. They wore light armor, and two of them carried javelins.

"Do the men of Gina stand with us today?" the Philistine asked.

The Hebrew soldier greeted him. "Yes we do, we certainly do."

Chapter Fourteen

"Saul and Jonathan *were* lovely and pleasant in their lives, and in their death they were not divided: they were swifter than eagles, they were stronger than lions."
II Samuel 1:23

Three Days Earlier: Ziklag

David and his mighty men walked through the town of Ziklag. David's alliance with Philistia had awarded him the vassal town, and for a brief period of time the men had homes for their wives and children.

The town had been attacked by the Amalekites. The Philistines, and David with them, had left many of their towns vulnerable by marching on Israel. Savagely the rovers had struck. Their homes were burnt and their wives and children taken. All around him David only saw the blackened and charred remains of his place of refuge.

Benaiah approached him, shaking with rage. "My wife, David. They've taken her. That Egyptian, the mercenary that fights with the Amalekites, he's been here. They've taken everything. Everything that matters."

David was distressed. His world was spinning out of control it seemed. Jonathan was on Gilboa, and David knew he was going to die. David's two wives had been taken. He could hear the rumbling of rebellion amongst his men.

Joab arrived. He was the son of David's sister, Zeruiah, but he hadn't gained his position of authority by simply being a nephew. Though about ten years younger than David he was as cunning a warrior and strategist as any man in his army.

"David, I suggest you do something and do it quickly," Joab said. "The married men want to stone you for this. They're blaming you and the alliance you have with the Philistines."

"That's ridiculous," Benaiah interrupted. "If David hadn't joined with—"

"No," David said, "They're right. I shouldn't have joined with the enemies of Israel. God said we're not to make a covenant with the people of the land, and I broke that. God let this happen."

"Sometimes things just happen," Benaiah said.

"No, they don't. Certainly things like this do not *just* happen. But God has mercy. God will forgive. He'll bring us back to our real homes again someday, men. We have to encourage ourselves in the LORD and in his promises."

"I mean no disrespect, David, but our men need action. Nice thoughts won't get them far," Joab said.

David looked to Abiathar, the priest, who hadn't said anything as of yet. "Bring forth the Ephod."

When David said that, Abiathar's mind went back to that terrible day. Saul and Doeg the Edomite were there. In the city of Nob the priests stood defiant towards the maniac king. Saul had been hunting David and he was enraged to learn that the priests had fed him and his troops. The order to slay the priests had been given, but the men of Israel stood paralyzed, unable to obey the ghastly command. Doeg and his men carried it out, but Abiathar had slipped into the tabernacle and escaped with the breastplate.

David spoke to the breastplate, the part of the ephod that contained the stones of Israel. "LORD, what would you have us to do? Should we pursue after them?"

The breastplate responded, the various stones lighting up in a pattern that made the message clear: *Pursue: for thou shalt surely overtake them, and without fail recover all.*

There was no time needed for preparation. David's mighty men were the greatest fighters of that time, but many of them were outcasts of Israel for good reasons. They were rough and hard men, having the faces of lions they would just as soon kill someone as afford him a second chance. Given too much time to consider their situation, some of these warriors would have turned on David.

They began a forced pursuit after the Amalekites. Through the dead of night they ran. Upon reaching the brook Besor, two-hundred of the men stayed behind. Their feet were cut and bleeding. They were exhausted and lacked the strength to go on. Even for men of this stature, David had literally run them into the ground in his pursuit of the rovers.

The other four-hundred mighty men continued on until they found a Egyptian slave that had been left by the Amalekites. After having been nourished back to health, the slave told David and his men where they could find the enemy.

The Amalekites were no match for David and his mighty men. Though they had travelled without sleep at astonishing speed, they attacked the sleeping camp like a wild bear bereaved of her whelps. The foolish marauders had been dancing and celebrating their raids against Judah and the Philistines when David struck them at twilight. The slaughter continued until the evening of the next day.

The families were restored. David instructed the men that the spoil was to be divided evenly between those that tarried by the stuff at Besor and those that fought.

And when the morning of the next day arrived, so did the news of Gilboa.

* * *

"We're about to be flanked," Saul said to Jonathan. "Prepare for a chariot assault. They'll be coming from the slope."

Jonathan turned to a battalion. "Slingers! Archers at the ready! Forward, on me!"

Several detachments followed the prince as he broke into a run heading towards the far south of Mount Gilboa. All of Mount Gilboa was a rocky ridge, save the gentle slopes of the southwest. Jonathan could see the chariots roaring up the slope, bouncing and jostling on the rough but manageable terrain.

Jonathan turned to his men. "You know what to do; we have to slow them down, harass them however we can until our heavy infantry can engage them."

The men immediately fanned out and began to advance towards the chariots, taking cover behind trees and boulders.

* * *

"Is this all there is?" an irate Saul said to the commander.

"Yes it is. There was none else to spare."

Saul's eyes turned glassy as he gazed across the mountainside. The men of Israel were fleeing from the Philistines. He was about to be flanked and all the preparation in the world had done nothing to save him. He knew the hand of the LORD was against him.

"Very well," Saul sighed. "Let's stop those chariots."

* * *

Rocks were peppering the terrain all around the chariots as they tore across the hillside. Still outside of chariot range, the Hebrew slingers were hurling the rocks from over four hundred yards away. In front of them, and sprinting forward, was Jonathan and a group of archers.

Jonathan turned to his brothers who were straggling behind him. "Brothers? Do you want to live forever? Live with courage; die with honor."

Still moving Jonathan notched an arrow and let it fly. The arrow soared high in the air and spiraling as it descended it brought a lead horse down, and the chariot tumbled forward. The riders spilled out, rolling across the ground. Dozens of chariots passed them by, with more on the way.

All the courage in the world isn't going to stop them, Jonathan thought.

The rocks kept falling from the sky, disrupting Philistine formations, but the chariots were closing the gap. The prince, a living legend of a sad and desperate people, climbed up a boulder to get a better view. Drawing the bowstring to his jaw he let arrow after arrow fly, every one of them hit their mark. They punctured breastplates and shattered helmets.

By now the chariots had come within range but something unexpected happened. They were shooting arrows as expected, but suddenly soldiers began jumping off the backs of the chariots. They hit the ground and rolled, and when they stood up they charged the archers with sword and shield.

"Treachery!" Jonathan yelled. Hopelessness choked his voice as his eyes teared up. Before him he saw the men of Gina, trained Hebrew soldiers, pouring out and attacking the archers. The archers scrambled to escape, but stood little chance. Jonathan's brothers were slain before his eyes.

"Oh God of my fathers, spare Israel this day," Jonathan said as he reached behind him for another arrow. The quiver was empty.

Jonathan slid off the boulder and hit the ground running. A swordsman charged him with his weapon held high. Perfectly enraged, Jonathan swung his bow like a club and knocked the man down. He ducked to avoid another sword, and retaliated by ramming the tip of the bow underneath the enemy's helmet. The prince roared like a bear and pulled a sword from one of his victims. He charged headlong into a group of ten men, weaving in and out of them he slew them all.

Jonathan looked before him and saw the chariots rolling up the hill towards Saul. He knew it was over. An arrow struck the ground near his feet, and when he looked up another one struck him in the chest. The prince fell to his knees as three more struck him, and the chariots rolled by.

Before the day was over, the Israelite army was shattered upon Gilboa, and Saul was dead. The bodies of Saul and his sons were taken by the Philistines and hung upon the wall of Beth-shan. It was the blessing of God at Gilgal that saved Saul's army and caused Hebrew mercenaries to turn on the Philistines that hired them. Conversely, it was the curse of God that allowed the opposite to take place on Mount Gilboa.

* * *

It didn't take long for the news to reach David. The Amalekite lied about Saul's death, hoping to please David by telling him he had finished him off. The truth was Saul had committed suicide in battle. David had the heathen slain for his story. David had refused to kill Saul several times when he had the opportunity, because he wasn't about to kill the LORD's anointed.

As the young men drug the body of the soldier away, David lifted up his voice and wept aloud. Those in the room with him, hardened soldiers and mercenaries, could barely contain themselves as he spoke the words.

"The beauty of Israel is slain upon thy high places: how are the mighty fallen!

"Tell *it* not in Gath, publish *it* not in the streets of Askelon; lest the daughters of the Philistines rejoice, lest the daughters of the uncircumcised triumph.

"Ye mountains of Gilboa, *let there be* no dew, neither *let there be* rain, upon you, nor fields of offerings: for there the shield of the mighty is vilely cast away, the shield of Saul, *as though he had* not *been* anointed with oil.

"From the blood of the slain, from the fat of the mighty, the bow of Jonathan turned not back, and the sword of Saul returned not empty.

"Saul and Jonathan *were* lovely and pleasant in their lives, and in their death they were not divided: they were swifter than eagles, they were stronger than lions.

"Ye daughters of Israel, weep over Saul, who clothed you in scarlet, with *other* delights, who put on ornaments of gold upon your apparel.

"How are the mighty fallen in the midst of the battle! O Jonathan, *thou wast* slain in thine high places.

"I am distressed for thee, my brother Jonathan: very pleasant hast thou been unto me: thy love to me was wonderful, passing the love of women.

"How are the mighty fallen, and the weapons of war perished!"

The men in the room wept with David. Not because they loved Saul; they all knew him for who he was. They wept not for Jonathan, though they respected him. They wept for David because they loved David.

They had followed David because he was a different kind of man. David didn't demand anything; he inspired men. They wanted to be like him, to fight like him and also to have the heart that he had. David had shown them failure, but he also had shown them repentance, success, and what waiting on God meant.

David had truly loved Jonathan more than anyone else. It was a love and kinship that was forged in combat and sorrow, a mutual admiration for each other; they had fought, fled and bled together and only those that have done that would understand that kind of love. Jonathan was older than David and was a mentor to him. Though David had the support of the greatest warriors on earth and the kingdom now lay before him for the taking, he felt very much alone.

* * *

In the dark of night four headless bodies hung from a stone wall, lighted only by the flickering of a small campfire. Three dead Philistines lay by that fire now, and a small detachment of Hebrew soldiers could be seen scaling the wall and removing the bodies of Saul and his sons. It was the men of Jabesh-Gilead. The men of the town that Saul protected from Nahash the Ammonite. The town of Jabesh-Gilead never forgot the kindness of

Saul to them. The kinship between them and the line of Benjamin was strong.

But the scepter belonged to Judah.

Chapter Fifteen

"With him *is* strength and wisdom: the deceived and the deceiver *are* his."
Job 12:16

The next day: the backside of Jupiter

Once again, the nation hung in the balance. And many times when something cataclysmic occurs in a nation, if one could see through the physical realm and into the spiritual, one might see a council like that which is occurring now at the planet Jupiter. For since the promise in the garden was given, Satan's goal had been to stop the arrival of the seed of the woman, and knowing that the seed was to come through this nation, he desired to destroy this nation.

"Gentlemen," Satan said to the small group of dark beings around him, "the king is dead, and long live the kings."

The other beings all muttered to each other and nodded their understanding.

Satan continued. "It is at times like these that we should take inventory of our situation. We have a split kingdom, but I fear it won't last too long. Though Ishbosheth, or perhaps I should say though Abner, rules the majority of Israel, David will not be ruled. He knows he is the anointed one, and he will not submit to the northern tribes though he may not force a war."

Alizel chimed in. "He won't have to; Joab will take care of that."

Satan smiled. "Ah yes, Joab, whatever shall we do with Joab? How he does like to step in and out of the shadows constantly."

"Joab and Abner are cut from the same mold," Alizel said.

"I wouldn't say that. Though they're both loyal to whoever will best suit their own personal agenda, Joab is ruthless. David knows it too, but he can't cut Joab off because he's too powerful in Judah and he's his nephew.

"Abner was there when Goliath fell, and he was there when David spared Saul time and time again. He knows what kind of man David is but he sought out this weak son of Saul to rule through. Setting up Ishbosheth when he should have gone to David will be his undoing, one way or another."

"What of Joab?" one of the other asked.

"As long as Joab stays loyal to David the blessings of God will trickle down to him."

Satan sighed and continued. "But my how Joab would make an excellent king."

"He'd ruin the kingdom in no time," Alizel said. "Cunning, merciless, unforgiving and conniving: why, he's a man after your own heart, my lord."

This was met with laughter all around and the Devil smiled and held his hand up.

"Thank-you. For now let us leave the matter of the two generals alone. They will both do what they will do, and will require absolutely no attention from us to accomplish it. They're like most people: they are their own worst enemies."

Satan turned to Wormwood. "My friend, what of the sun and moon gods?"

"The sun god is strong north of Israel and the moon god is strong south of Israel. Both have operated underground within Israel, but even under Saul idolatry was kept at a bare minimum. I can't even imagine what it will be like under David. If the people get a taste of his passion for Jehovah, we'll be set back for generations."

"Don't give up the fight. When this kingdom is finally split there will be a religious split with it, because there will *have* to be for the nations to remain politically separate."

Wormwood nodded. "Divide and conquer."

"Exactly, which brings us back to the son of Jesse. I want everything we can thrown at him. With Jonathan gone, I don't see any other man that can save the kingdom. If David falls, Israel falls with him.

"David will utilize his feigned alliance with the Philistines to get them to pull back, or perhaps to even bolster his own numbers in the certain-to-occur war between himself and Ishbosheth. The fools will play right along. He'll turn on them once he's united the kingdom under himself."

Alizel interrupted. "Joab's not the only shrewd one."

Satan continued. "No he's not. I want everything thrown on him: lust for power or women, fear of man, pride, anything and everything. Exploit any weakness at the first opportunity. He is the key to this whole thing. We destroy him and we destroy everything.

"It's been nothing but blood, guts and hair up to this point, and we're just getting started: it's time to wreck a kingdom."

If one could look north, up and past Alpha Draconis and through the sea of glass, right into the throne room of God, one would see the LORD turn to Michael and speak the words, "It's time to *spread* a kingdom."

Chapter Sixteen

"And the king said unto his servants, Know ye not that there is a prince and a great man fallen this day in Israel?"
II Samuel 3:38

Two Years Later: Hebron

There was nothing soft, sloppy or undisciplined about him. He walked at no-nonsense pace, which was a keen reflection of how he did everything in life. The young man's eyes were narrow and shifty, his tanned face pock-marked, and his jaw was firm. His leather armor fit perfectly and the blood had been cleanly wiped off his polished sword. A hundred Hebrew soldiers followed him with sacks over their shoulders containing captured treasure and weapons.

War is a great racket, Joab thought.

The people of Hebron cleared a path as they walked down the street, and the wives of the soldiers came out to greet them. It didn't take long for Joab to hear the news that Abner had been there while they were out.

Joab spoke to Abishai in hushed tones. "What of Abner?"

"He's met with David. Apparently he wants peace. He's also returned Michael to him."

Joab cursed. "We can't have peace yet; Abner's still alive."

"You can't say that to the king, brother."

"I swore that man would die for Asahel, and he's going to die. David is soft; he's always been soft. Adding a third wife is just going to make him softer. Abner needs to die. If he doesn't he'll just cause problems. The power of the kingdom must remain with Judah."

"I agree, brother. Do what you must."

It didn't take long for Joab to confront David. The king ruled in Hebron, but the throne room wasn't anything to be considered overtly regal or impressive. It was a large room with some tables and a raised wooden throne. It was functional, not opulent.

"My lord, the king," Joab said to David.

"What of the pursuit?" David returned.

"One less Amalekite raiding party to harass us, and quite a bit of treasure and weapons for the men."

"I appreciate how well a job you've done training the conscripts," David said.

"They learn fast,"

David smiled. "What you mean is they learn fast or else."

"Can't argue with results, can you?" Joab snorted, not returning the smile.

Joab was never in a good mood per se, but David could tell there was something else hiding beneath the rough exterior of his general.

"What is it, Joab?"

Joab didn't hesitate to speak freely. "I'm out fighting for the kingdom and you're holding a feast behind my back with our enemy? You sent him away without hearing my counsel? You can't trust Abner. He's power hungry. He's only here to spy out our situation and find a weak spot. He's manipulating you!"

"I think you have him wrong. Abner is solid. He returned Michael to me and he's looking to unify the kingdom. We'll be a united kingdom again, Joab, isn't that great?"

"He'll use you like he's using Ishbosheth, David!"

David's face hardened and he leaned forward in the throne. "You listen to me, Joab. When I desire your consultation on matters of state, I'll ask for it. You're compromised on this one; you and I both know it. This has nothing to do with the kingdom and everything to do with Asahel. You have to let it go. Abner slew him on the battlefield and you know he even warned him. Your brother was a good man, a mighty man, but he knew the risks when he tangled with Abner. The war is over."

Joab snorted, thumped his chest in salute, turned and stormed out of the room. The general seethed with every step he took down the dirt road. For Joab there was no time of indecision or contemplation. Nearing the city gates, he found a runner and dispatched him to request that Abner return.

Hours later, Abner lay dead in the gate of Hebron; Joab had murdered him.

* * *

There was no conspiracy made by David to cover Joab's crime. Early in the morning David followed the funeral procession with the family members who were present. Through the streets and outside of the town it went as Abner's body was carried on a wooden plank. His eyes and mouth had been securely closed and his body anointed with oil. It was a long procession; people sobbed and wailed loudly, threw dust in the air, tore their clothing and musicians played. Once the body was placed in the rock hewn tomb, David took the initiative to say a few words.

He didn't pull any punches. Everyone knew what had happened, but many were shocked that the king would publically acknowledge it. "Died Abner as a fool dieth?"

He turned and faced the tomb, and continued speaking. "Thy hands were not bound, nor thy feet put into fetters: as a man falleth before wicked men, so fellest thou.

"A great man has been buried today, O Israel. Weep and mourn for thine son Abner."

This wasn't simply a case of a politician saying something nice at the right time; Abner's death affected David the entire day. He refused to eat, and whenever a servant would come to him with official business, it was usually delayed until another time.

"Know ye not that a prince is fallen this day?" David would say, and the servant would shirk back. It became very clear to all of Israel what kind of man David was, and that his hands were clean of the blood of Abner.

Towards the end of the day Joab and Abishai came before him. The two men had run the army with an iron fist over the last two years and were incredibly popular with the people of Judah. All of David's court was there as he addressed them.

"Ye sons of Zeruiah are too hard for me. There has been enough death today and though I am king, I am weak. I'm not going to have you executed for Abner, God shall be your judge. Ye have done wickedness, and may the LORD reward the doer of evil according to his wickedness."

Both men left the throne room of David guilty, though only one had actually performed the act. In David's mind Abishai was guilty as well because he had approved of what Joab was going to do. Neither one had been forgiven, though they were allowed a second chance. Both had been publically humbled, and only time would tell how they would respond to David's verbal chastisement.

David was eventually anointed king over all Israel. Ishbosheth had been murdered in his sleep, and David showed himself again to be the type of man that didn't approve of wickedness. The men who killed Ishbosheth were themselves killed, just as the Amalekite that claimed to have killed Saul on David's behalf was executed.

The kingdom was united behind David, and the Philistines were fooled into thinking they had some sort of control over him. Though they had won a tremendous battle at Mount Gilboa years earlier, they had backed off and supported David during the civil war.

That was now all about to change, because David was going to do something that would transform the entire landscape of the Middle East.

Chapter Seventeen

"Our feet shall stand within thy gates, O Jerusalem."
Psalm 122:2

1048 B.C. Hebron

"This will bring the wrath of the Philistines down upon us," Abishai said.

"Let it come. I'm tired of pretending to be their friends," Joab said in his customary snort.

"Tell us again why it's so important," Eliazar said, with a knowing smile.

"Well," David began, "Jebus is centrally located. It is on major roads and arteries that head every direction, and as such it is preferable for trade. It will connect our kingdom as it needs to be, and provide a fortress that can efficiently respond to an invasion from any side. It is set upon a ridge that makes it easy to defend as well. Because it belongs to the Jebusites, we won't have any tribal political issues to deal with once we take it. It will be a perfect capital for our united kingdom."

Eliazar understood that David knew the scripture, and he knew there was more to what was going on here. He smiled and said, "Tell us why you *really* think it's important, my king."

David let out a sigh, and smiled as well. "Well, there's no place like Jerusalem. Do you remember that unusual man that met with our father Abraham so long ago? His name was Melchizedek, and he was the king of Salem. I don't know what that man talked about when he broke bread with our father; but if I had to guess, it had something to do about this kingdom we're trying to spread."

David continued, and by now he was becoming very excited and his voice grew stronger. "Men, we must never forget we are the army of the LORD of hosts. I believed it when I slew the giant, and I believe it still today. I may be king, but the real king is the captain of the LORD's host that met Joshua that day.

"Job talked about standing in his flesh after worms had eaten his body! Do you understand that? He was talking about a resurrection, and Job's been dead for a very long time! He said that he would see the LORD actually stand upon the earth, just like Joshua and Moses saw him, and that it would be after he had been resurrected. He said he knew his redeemer lived and that he'd stand in the latter day upon the earth.

"This is my hope, men! My hope is that we are right now in the latter day that Job spoke of, and that the redeemer will come now. I've been writing about it and singing about it my whole life. Maybe, just maybe, by taking Jerusalem, by taking this Zion, it will trigger the events that are needed for the king to come."

David went on and on, quoting the prophesies he had written in his songs. He took a deep breath and just looked at them. Some gave a knowing smile, some smirked like they couldn't care less, some had a blank expression on their faces, and then there was Joab. Joab had an alternative view of the end times and was pretty proud of his uniqueness.

David saw the look on Joab's face and relented. "Okay Joab, what is it?"

"Well, Your Majesty, you're honestly the only king I'm looking forward to. I've read those passages that you're talking about, and I fail to see what you're seeing. I think you're over-literalizing it a bit."

David cocked his head and smiled, and the other men in the room raised their eyebrows. "Over-literalizing it, Joab?"

"Well yes, actually I do. You see that passage about Moses you love to cling to, the one where he speaks of the LORD coming with ten thousands of his saints?"

"Yes, that's a good one," David said.

Joab continued. "Well, that prophecy has already been fulfilled. That's the same one that Enoch spoke of, and it was fulfilled when the people took the land under Moses and Joshua."

"Oh, I see," David said.

"Yes, actually, and another one that you tend to use is that one where it asks 'who can count the dust of Jacob, and number the fourth part of Israel?' That doesn't mean there's some sort of fantasy golden age in our future, it just means that one day we'll have a great nation, as we do now. All those prophesies that you cling to have already been fulfilled."

"That's the silliest thing I've ever heard," David replied.

Joab continued to speak, but now with his eyes closed. "Well, many of the greatest scholars agree that that we are currently living in the golden age and that the redeemer is spiritually ruling over the Earth—"

"Currently living in the golden age? That's ridiculous! Why the king is coming, and when he does, he's going to live among us! Why else did God promise that there would be the seed of a woman, and why did Jacob say that this Shiloh would gather all the people together?

"How in the world are all families of the Earth being blessed by us right now? We're practically running out or even wiping out anyone who gets in our way. There is a golden age coming and we're going to do everything we can to bring it in! Once we take all the land the seed will come."

David never seemed to take a breath as he continued on. "You quoted Balaam, a scoundrel much like yourself if you don't mind me saying so, and yet you failed to mention that little part where he said, 'I shall see him, but not now: I shall behold him, but not nigh: there shall come a Star out of Jacob, and a Sceptre shall rise out of Israel'."

Everyone stood there quietly, just looking at the table. The king had spoken *very* passionately, and most were a little nervous to question him.

"Well?" David said, his eyes scanning the room.

Towards the back of the room one man poked his hand up. It was Benaiah, the lion killer. He had faced down and killed an Egyptian giant at the battle of Ziklag, taking the man's own spear way from him and slaying him with it. Benaiah was a good man, but not generally known as one who knew the scriptures all that well.

"Well," Benaiah began, "Joab is saying over here that there isn't a future golden age because we're living it right now, and you're over here saying that seed will come after we take the land. What if us taking the land has nothing to do with the coming kingdom? What if the king will come when he wants to and after that, and only after that, will we get all the land that was promised to Abraham?"

David stroked his beard. "Hmmm. What would that be? Some sort of pre-kingdom theology?"

"That's right," Benaiah said.

"That's silly," David said.

"Absolutely absurd," Joab grunted.

"Bizarre," Abishai added.

"Strange and heretical if you ask me," Eliazar said.

"That's enough," David interrupted, "Benaiah can believe whatever he wants to about the coming king, but now that we're done scratching the fourth wall I suggest we get down to business."

And with that David explained to the men how they were going to take the Jebusite fortess of Jerusalem.

Chapter Eighteen

"And the king and his men went to Jerusalem unto the Jebusites, the inhabitants of the land: which spake unto David, saying, Except thou take away the blind and the lame, thou shalt not come in hither: thinking, David cannot come in hither."
II Samuel 5:6

A Week Later; Jerusalem

Joab and the mighty men stood with the Kidron Valley to their backs and the walls of Jerusalem before them. Beside him stood Benaiah.

"Simple enough plan," Benaiah said, "Provided one of us actually survives it."

Joab saw the situation as a seasoned soldier; Jerusalem was not a soft target. It was the finest example of military fortifications he had ever seen. Protected on three sides by steep slopes only minor defenses were needed to protect the city.

"I can see why they said they could hold the city with only the sick and the lame," Joab said.

Benaiah scratched the back of his head. "Yes, I can see why the Philistines have left them alone for so long, and why we have as well."

"They have about a thousand armed men in there. That's about enough for every Jebusite to stand at arm's length from each other. David seems to think that he can just bash his way in with superior numbers."

"I think David knows what he's doing, Joab. We have the numbers, and if our men are constantly shifting positions we're at a seven-to-one advantage. It seems easy enough—"

"Nothing about this is going to be easy," Joab interrupted. "David is going to lose half his army because he won't listen to me."

"Then prove him wrong," Benaiah said. "You want to run this army, then prove him wrong. He said the first on the wall is general from hereon out."

Joab's anger rose within him. "I should already be general of this army! I proved myself a dozen times over! When Abner died, I should have been reinstated."

Benaiah was unimpressed as he turned to walk away. "Yes, Joab, and how did he die? How did he die?"

* * *

The men of Israel moved towards the walls from all sides. David had suggested many ideas but left it to the leaders within his army to decide their own path. David needed a new general and he wanted a man that could think on his own and improvise if needed.

Various tactics were being used: companies were executing feint attacks to keep the defenders constantly moving from area to area, others were unsuccessfully attempting to build a ramp to climb the wall, and some were climbing the wall as it was.

* * *

Joab paced outside the wall, angrily muttering to himself. His brother Abishai stood a short distance off, watching. Joab stopped, pausing momentarily; he watched as a small, virtually unnoticeable, stream of water flowed over his foot. He looked up at Abishai, "Follow me."

* * *

The walls of the city were constructed of rough-hewn, ill-fitting blocks of stone with the spaces between the stones filled with rubble. Every six courses of stone the wall receded back so as to form steps several feet in height and six inches deep. Some of the Israelites were managing to climb the wall as it was, and David and several other slingers were providing cover.

From the top of the wall, the Jebusite archers were picking off his men. David and his slingers fired back, but the archers were well placed and difficult to target. The climb was long, arduous and hazardous; anytime a Hebrew would actually make it onto the wall he was struck down.

David saw the situation and understood it clearly: he had underestimated the forces at Jerusalem and while his men were fearsome hand-to-hand fighters they lacked the tactical understanding necessary to secure victory. There were no generals among them.

David saw defeat all around him. The men were falling from the walls, struck down by the enemies' arrows. Some struggled back to their feet and valiantly attempted to climb the wall again. Other lay still, the vacant look of death on their faces. Some of the able-bodied were helping the injured limp away to safety, the blood soaking through their clothing. They screamed in agony and frustration, and the sound rattled David for a moment. *O keep my soul, and deliver me: let me not be ashamed; for I put my trust in thee. Let integrity and uprightness preserve me; for I wait on thee. Redeem Israel, O God, out of all his troubles.*

* * *

"The army can't get in but water can? That's your plan? Those archers will take us down before we reach it," Abishai said to his brother.

"We don't have much of a choice," Joab replied. "The men will die if we don't try it."

Abishai looked at the guards on the wall, and then his vision went down to the base of the wall. Joab and Abishai had followed the water flow to the city and found the entry point. It was crudely disguised behind some rubble and shrubs, but both of them knew there was a way into the city there.

Abishai looked back at Joab. "Don't tell me you care about the men enough to lose your life. I know you better than that."

Joab sighed. "If David loses this battle we lose the kingdom. It's as simple as that. By just trying to take Jerusalem we'll awaken the Sea Filth, and we'll be too disorganized and demoralized to fight back."

"So this is political?"

Joab smiled. "Are politics, courage, and nobleness always mutually exclusive?"

Abishai was about to reply, but something caught his eye. The sky had appeared dreary and overcast all day, but now a dense fog was rolling in. It came in fast and completely obscured the city.

God had answered David's prayer.

Abishai and Joab crouched low as they silently moved towards the wall, all the while following the trickle of water towards the city. Quietly they squeezed their way through the water passageway and into the dark corridor. They were inside of a stone passageway, a gutter of some kind that ran vertically through the inside of the wall. Clinging to the walls they saw a pool of water below them.

Abishai looked up and saw the daylight above them. "We're in a well."

Joab whispered as he climbed up the shaft. "You've got a keen grasp of the obvious. Keep your voice down; watch the echo."

They heard voices coming from above them and stopped their ascent. Looking up they saw a few torches illuminate the shaft, and the two brothers hugged the wall and looked down. The guard shouted and started throwing rocks down at them.

Joab grunted as a rock the size of his head struck his shoulder. Abishai pulled his shield off his back and handed it up to Joab. Quickly they ascended the shaft as the men at the entrance dropped debris upon them, while Joab used the shield to protect them.

They were nearly to the top when a thick, black liquid slopped down on the shield and spilled off onto Abishai.

"That's pitch!" Joab yelled as he saw the torch fall. It hit the shield and set it ablaze. Abishai sprung to the other side and clung to it as Joab dropped the shield to the water below. *No pagan is going to kill another brother of mine today,* he thought.

The men at the top drew their spears. Abishai grunted as his hand slipped and then regriped a rock. "Too bad they don't throw those; it would make this a lot easier."

"Their weaponry isn't necessary," Joab said as he reached behind his back; he drew out several long razor-sharp darts. "I find these to be handy from time to time." Joab threw the darts and the three guards stumbled backwards, gasping and reeling.

The brothers sprung out and onto the wall. Abishai ducked low and sidestepped as a Jebusite charged him. Joab in turn kicked him into the watershaft. Both men looked at each other, and then the screaming mob of Jebusites that were now charging them. Abishai shrugged his shoulders and drew his sword.

* * *

The men of Israel had used the opportunity of the fog to pull back. David was speaking to the mighty men now and the other soldiers were listening and tending to their wounded.

"We outnumber them; we simply need to create a breach," David said. "I want you to use the fog to scout the base of the wall. Search for anything, a passage, a waterway, something. There has to be a way in. If you find a gutter or waterway, the first one up commands the army."

Just then, David heard a very loud *thud* sound. It came from the city. It was followed by a couple more *thuds* and some screams. The fog cleared and David looked up on the wall in time to see another man falling off the wall, a spear through his belly.

"Where's Joab?" David blurted.

Benaiah smiled. "I think he's on the wall."

Under the fog of war, it didn't take David and his men long to ascend the wall and join Joab and Abishai to win the day. From that day and forward, Jerusalem would be known as the city of David, and as irony would have it, the word Jerusalem meant the last thing anyone would ever think the place to be: the city of peace.

Chapter Nineteen

"Even as David also describeth the blessedness of the
man, unto whom God imputeth righteousness without
works,"
Romans 4:6

1044 B.C. Jerusalem

As David walked through the twilight of night, the words of the LORD rang in his mind. *Thou hast shed blood abundantly, and hast made great wars: thou shalt not build an house unto my name, because thou hast shed much blood upon the earth in my sight.*

It was the greatest disappointment in David's life. David was a legendary warrior capable of taking on scores of men at a time. He was a giant killer. His presence on the battlefield alone inspired the troops as nothing else would, and they would follow him into the jaws of death if he ordered it.

But unlike his nephew Joab, that's not what he loved. He didn't love violence. That's not what he wanted. David wanted peace, he wanted to be out somewhere alone on a hillside playing a song and watching sheep. He didn't want to kill, but that's what the LORD required of him. Like Joshua before him, he was the sword of God's judgment. Because of that very fact, God would not allow him to fulfill his heart's content: build a permanent temple for the LORD.

The words that Nathan brought him continued in his mind. *Shalt thou build me an house for me to dwell in? Whereas I have not dwelt in any house since the time that I brought up the children of Israel out of Egypt, even to this day, but have walked in a tent and in a tabernacle. In all the places wherein I have walked with all the children of Israel spake I a word with any of the tribes of Israel, whom I commanded to feed my people Israel, saying, Why build ye not me an house of cedar?*

David wasn't angry at this. He didn't feel as though he'd been cheated out of anything, but he was sorely disappointed in what God's will was for his life. He felt as though he was designed to do something else other than what he was asked to do.

A lot had happened in the four years that had passed from the battle of Jerusalem. The Philistines attacked twice, and twice they were beaten. It was a devastating defeat for the Sea People, and holing up in their cities they did not attempt another campaign. The hand of God was on David, and when David led the people into battle they simply did not lose. He may not have had the strategic mind of Joab or Saul, but he didn't need it.

David had peace on all sides now, and had believed now was as good a time as any to build a temple unto the LORD. But that wasn't what was on his mind at the moment. There was something else that Nathan had said that was bothering him; he wasn't able to understand it, to put it together.

Peering through the darkness, he saw the fence surrounding the tabernacle. He passed through the gate, heading east to west, and the first thing he saw was the flames of the brazen altar. They reminded him of the fire of God's wrath and holiness. They spoke to him of the afterlife of the enemies of God.

David was barefoot now, and slowly he walked towards the altar. Prayerfully and penitently he grabbed the horns of the altar. He believed touching the horns would make him holy.

After a moment, David turned and faced the tabernacle door. Between him and the door stood the brasen laver. It spoke to him of purification, and that none might approach God unclean. David walked past the laver and sat on the ground facing the door of the tabernacle. Going any further would have meant instant death, for only a Levitical priest was allowed to enter the holy place. But David went as close as he could to the presence of God, to the Ark of the Covenant.

God had reaffirmed that Israel was his people. He reaffirmed his promise of a kingdom for them, and that they would all dwell in the land safely.

Moreover I will appoint a place for my people Israel, and will plant them, that they may dwell in a place of their own, and move no more; neither shall the children of wickedness afflict them any more, as beforetime.

This was comforting to David, but it wasn't new revelation. It was for what he had been fighting from the moment he took Goliath's head. His life was about spreading the kingdom and taking the land that had been promised to Moses and Joshua. He believed that if he could just take the land, then the peace that was promised would follow.

But that wasn't what was getting at him. God had said something new, and the Holy Spirit that anointed him and guided him battle after battle was speaking to him again. That spirit that guided him as he wrote and fought told him there was a deeper revelation to be had here.

David sat in the silence, and pondered the word of the LORD. *I will set up thy seed after thee, and I will establish his kingdom. He shall build an house for my name, and I will stablish the throne of his kingdom for ever.*

"Who am I, O Lord GOD?" David said, "And what is my house, that thou hast brought me hitherto? And this was yet a small thing in thy sight, O Lord GOD; but thou hast spoken also of thy servant's house for a great while to come."

God had told David that he wouldn't come to the same end as Saul. The children of Judah, the line of David, would rule the kingdom forever. David's son would forever have the mercy of God upon his life, as would David himself.

But my mercy shall not depart away from him, as I took it from Saul, whom I put away before thee. He shall build an house for my name, and I will stablish the throne of his kingdom for ever. I will be his father, and he shall be my son.

David didn't want to consider the implications of what God meant when he removed his mercy from Saul. Whether God spoke of the temporal and the eternal together wasn't clear concerning the maniac king, but what was clear was that David and his son had something that was unheard of to him and his people:

the eternal imputed righteousness and mercy of God almighty.

David looked behind him at the brasen altar and trembled at the thought that it wasn't needed. "How is it even possible?" he whispered. *The blood, there has to be the blood. Without shedding of blood, there is no remission. The atonement, the forgiveness, it comes from the death of the innocent in my place.*

David knew the scriptures like no one else alive at that time. He knew the account of the garden written by Moses. His mind replayed the stories of the LORD appearing in human form to men like Joshua and Abraham. He remembered the story of a man in the land of Uz who cried out in anguish for his dead family. The same man made a statement that had forever haunted David: *For he is not a man, as I am, that I should answer him, and we should come together in judgment. Neither is there any daysman betwixt us, that might lay his hand upon us both.*

A divine revelation was beginning to form within the mind of David. He wasn't able to piece it together; he didn't know how it worked. He saw through a glass darkly, but he knew that something had happened to him, that he had a certain promise of eternity.

As the tears streamed down his face, David uttered the words, "I will behold thy face in righteousness: I shall be satisfied, when I awake, with thy likeness." He must have looked like Abraham that day as he gazed into the stars rejoicing in the righteousness God had given him.

Before turning to walk away, David thanked the LORD one last time. "Blessed are they whose iniquities are forgiven, and whose sins are covered. Blessed is the man to whom the Lord will not impute sin."

Chapter Twenty

**"And on this manner did Absalom to all Israel that
came to the king for judgment: so Absalom stole the
hearts of the men of Israel."**
II Samuel 15:6

1023 B.C. Jerusalem

Satan was relentless and tireless. His endgame
was always the same: prevent the arrival of the
seed of the woman. To do that, he must
destroy the people by which the seed must come. To
destroy the people, he must destroy the kingdom. To
destroy the kingdom, he must take down the king.

Taking down Saul wasn't nearly the challenge that
David was proving to be.

David had been ruling for thirty-two years now; he
was sixty-two years old. David had lived on the run
from Saul, never giving into carnal pride and slaying
God's anointed. After becoming king in Hebron, David
had endured a civil war and kept himself humble before
the LORD the entire time. David always had the correct
heart attitude regardless of what was placed before him.

God had given David a special unconditional
covenant reaffirming the land he promised to Abraham.
Furthermore, he was promised that it would be of his
seed that the Messiah would come, and that he and his
son would forever have the sure mercies of David.

Following that promise, David went to war on all
sides. He knew God was with him, and he had a

kingdom to spread. The hated Philistines finally had been subdued. They would never again attempt to invade Israel. David launched campaigns against the Syrians, the Edomites, Ammonites, and the Moabites. David pursued and all but annihilated the Amalekites, as was commanded to Saul; but a small faction of them managed to escape.

David had not taken all of the land promised to Abraham, but the kingdom had never been stronger.

In spite of all of these victories, Satan had not abandoned his plan to destroy the kingdom. Unable to affect David by the pride of life, Satan moved against him with the lust of the flesh. Weakened by carnal desires outside of God's will, David multiplied unto himself wives and concubines. The day came when that wasn't enough and he committed adultery with Bathsheba, the wife of one of his own mighty men. To cover up the incident, David had Uriah slain in battle and then he married Bathsheba.

The days were dark and it looked as though Satan had finally found the way to destroy David. The adversary railed against the Almighty with accusations and demanded that David be slain for this transgression. *He defiled a man's wife, committed murder, and then lied about it to cover it up!* With David gone, Satan believed the kingdom would fall back into darkness and crumble. God sent Nathan to rebuke David, and He told Satan that if David failed to repent he could kill him on the spot.

Have mercy upon me, O God, according to thy lovingkindness: according unto the multitude of thy tender mercies blot out my transgressions.

David repented. Bathsheba repented. Fellowship was restored. For his rebuke, David loved and appreciated Nathan so much that he would eventually name one of his sons after him. David and Bathsheba lost their first son together, but the LORD blessed them with another that they named Solomon. The trial and chastening brought David and Bathsheba closer together.

The kingdom had been spared by David's repentance, but dark days lay ahead and it would once again fall into jeopardy. David had unwittingly spoken his own punishment: *he shall restore the lamb fourfold, because he did this thing, and because he had no pity.*

David would lose four family members because of his sin. The first lamb to die was David and Bathsheba's firstborn son. The innocent baby died because of David's sin.

The second lamb was Amnon, another one of David's sons. A terrible incestuous scandal rocked the kingdom and David turned a blind eye to it. Absalom took matters into his own hands and murdered Amnon, and then he fled for his life. Of all people, Joab took the task upon himself to bring Absalom back to the kingdom.

Absalom was the son of David's wife named Maacah, who was the daughter of a king of wild Syrian tribe known as the Geshurites. David had married the woman during the Hebrew civil war. Absalom was by far the most popular of David's sons: people were glad he had done something about the Amnon situation. Absalom had a natural charm about him; people admired him. Men respected him because though he lacked battle experience, he had been trained with the best for combat and could take care of himself. Women adored him because he was tall, attractive, and as yet unspoken for. It was a joke among the women that they wished they had hair as thick and beautiful as his.

When Joab had brought Absalom back home, David shunned him. David found himself in a difficult place: his son that was guilty of rape was murdered by another one of his sons, which only complicated the whole ordeal. Now Absalom was guilty as well, and David knew the law: *ye shall take no satisfaction for the life of a murderer, which is guilty of death: but he shall be surely put to death.* David refused to put Absalom to death because he knew he himself was guilty of the same thing. David's response to the entire situation was to ignore it. David didn't even see Absalom for two years until the wild Bedouin child burned Joab's fields and forced David to admit him.

David was old and weak in the eyes of the people; he lacked the will and strength to lead. He had become lackluster and detached from the needs of the people. The glory days were becoming a memory.

Absalom took upon himself the mantle of leadership and began to gather unto himself a following. He was involved in behind-the-scenes subterfuge and intrigue, and he always came out smelling like a rose. He drew crowds and spoke to people sympathetically. He seemed to have time for everyone, and he seemed to be everyone's best friend. Absalom was very subtle: he spoke with leading questions and half-truths. He was very good at revealing problems, only the solutions he advised were always vague and usually just reflected having attitudes and abstract ideas of acceptance for a bright and different tomorrow. Love for David had become silly and passé, and everyone understood that Absalom was the future of the kingdom, and that with him as leader the kingdom looked bright.

David, who now had a rebellion on his hands, was completely paralyzed to the entire situation.

Chapter Twenty-One

**"And Ruth said, Intreat me not to leave thee, *or* to
return from following after thee: for whither thou
goest, I will go; and where thou lodgest, I will lodge:
thy people *shall be* my people, and thy God my
God:
Where thou diest, will I die, and there will I be buried:
the LORD do so to me, and more also, *if ought* but
death part thee and me."
Ruth 1:16-17**

B eniah looked at the men before him and felt
his beard. "You men come from a long way."
The man in front regarded Beniah with an
almost distant look in his eye. "We heard those
discouraged, in debt, or in distress could join the lord of
these lands. We come to offer our services."

Normally in a situation like this Beniah would chide
the would-be mercenary standing before him, but not
today. The Hebrew warrior saw experience in these
vagabonds that didn't necessitate it.

"You're from Gath then? Are you Philistines, come
to join your enemy?"

The leader took a step forward. "We are exiles. My
name is Ittai, and I lead these men. If you will have me,
my name will live forever in your writings of history."

* * *

In another meeting, only a few hours later that day, Absalom smiled at the group of men he had before him. "Hello, gentlemen. I'm here to discuss the obvious with you: the kingdom is mine. The people want something different from what they've had, and that's what I've offered them. Taking the throne will merely be a formality, and it can be done with or without bloodshed. It is for this reason that I ask you all to join me. None of us here want bloodshed."

Abishai shifted in his seat, and Joab grunted. "I've been shedding blood all my life, boy."

Absalom turned to them. "Yes, you have, haven't you? Have you noticed how soft the king has become? Why are the Ammonites allowed to continue? We have all these nations under subjection, but don't you think some of them would be much easier to manage if they simply weren't around to manage?"

The thought didn't even faze Joab. "You mean annihilation?"

Absalom ran a hand through his thick hair. "Abraham was promised all this land. Saul was told to annihilate the Amalekites. Joshua was told to run the nations out, and yet they keep creeping back."

Absalom's vision danced quickly from person to person concerning the seed he had just planted, so he decided to shift the direction of the thought he was putting forth. "Joab, I'm not suggesting annihilating anyone. I'm simply making the point that my father has become soft in his old age, and there's still much land to be taken. The army needs more men; we need better security; and we need to spread the kingdom."

Abishai looked over at Joab. "Hard to argue with that."

Absalom clasped his hands together and then released them to emphasize his next point. "If blood be shed, let it not be Hebrew blood. Join me, and we'll make sure that doesn't happen."

Absalom continued to appeal to the other individuals in the room, one by one. To Zadok, the priest, he rehashed all of David's failures and the lives that were lost because of it. Zadok countered by reminding Absalom of Amnon.

"There is no evidence that I had anything to do with the death of my brother," Absalom retorted. "God has judged and punished the king's family because of his moral failures. That is why Amnon is dead today."

The room grew silent.

"The fact is, gentlemen, the throne will be mine tomorrow. I have the army in tow. The people support me, and most of David's own court has joined me."

Absalom's face hardened and his eyes narrowed. "I met with one of David's chief advisors, Ahithophel, today. As I'm sure you're all aware, Ahithophel is Bathsheba's grandfather. I reminded him of what customarily occurs to the family of deposed kings, and I offered to provide him protection and grace. He will continue to serve as he always has before, only now in my court.

"I'm making you all the same offer. I don't want bloodshed. I want progress and I want peace within Israel."

* * *

"Your Majesty, Absalom is out for blood. He will simply not be satiated," Hushai the Archite said. Hushai was a personal friend of David's. He was much older than he and also served as one of the king's counselors.

"That's right, David, if you want the throne, you're going to have to fight for it," Joab said.

"No, no, no, no," David kept repeating as he walked. He raised his index finger up to Joab's face as his voice came to a crescendo. "I'm not going to fight my own boy! You sons of Zeruiah wear me out with the constant killing!"

Joab's face turned red with anger and Hushai stepped in between him and David. "Your Majesty, it's not a matter of whether or not we want blood. You don't have a choice in the matter."

David's eyes were fierce. "I do have a choice; I'm not going to fight my son."

"Then we'll have to flee, my lord. If we're not going to fight, we'll have to flee. Absalom will come here and kill us all."

David looked to the mighty men that were in the room with him. He was asking them to do the last thing in the world that they wanted to do. Beniah was the first to speak. "Behold, thy servants are ready to do whatsoever my lord the king doth appoint."

That night the king abdicated the kingdom and the throne of Jerusalem was empty the next morning.

Throughout the night David and his men journeyed towards the Mount of Olives and across the Jordan River.

Zadok the priest who came to join David and the others, bore with him the Ark of the Covenant. David sent Zadok back to Jerusalem. "Take the Ark back. If the LORD desires to return me to the throne then so be it. The Ark belongs in Jerusalem."

The king walked up the Mount of Olives barefoot with his head covered. The men that followed him did the same, weeping. Hushai came to the king with dirt upon his head, weeping. The king sent him back to Jerusalem as well.

Sometime along the way another group of people came to join the king. This group of people was very unusual. They weren't Hebrew soldiers. All the Hebrews had joined up with Absalom; he had stolen away the hearts of the men of Israel. They weren't the mighty men; those men were already expected to follow David to the ends of the Earth, and surely they would.

As David looked to the west, he saw a group of about six hundred men advancing upon him. Their armour was random and so was their weaponry. There was nothing standardized or regular about any of them. It was clear that every stitch of armour had a reason, and every nook in every weapon handle had a purpose. Simply put, they were very seasoned for war and had customized their armament quite well.

When David saw them, he stopped. The leader of the men came upon him and stood before him as the rest passed on in the direction that David and his men were already headed. David watched as the men walked on past him, and he was surprised to see among them some little children.

David turned to face their leader. "Why are going with us? Return to your own place. Go back to where you came from. This isn't your fight."

The man said nothing. He just looked at David and blinked. David was exasperated. "I said go back. You're a stranger and an exile. You came here when, just yesterday? You're not even Hebrew, are you? Return to your own land and to your own people. I'm not about to force a mercenary, with children nonetheless, to follow me to the wilderness and back."

David paused and waited for a response, and then went on. "I mean, you can't follow me. I don't really know where I'm headed. I don't have anything really to pay you with. Return, take your brethren and little ones back to the land from which you came."

There was a moment of silence between them, and David looked at the man. "Mercy and truth be with thee."

Once it was clear that David had nothing left to say, the stranger spoke the following words to the king of Israel. "As the LORD liveth, and as my lord the king liveth, surely in what place my lord the king shall be, whether in death or life, even there also will thy servant be."

The words nearly took David's breath away and nearly caused him to weep on the spot. To David, here was a dirty, Gentile dog. He was a Gittitte, a man who had come from Goliath's territory of Gath. He could have been a Philistine for all David knew. David wouldn't have given the time of day to a man like this a week ago, and yet this mercenary had chosen to follow him. The purebred pride and lineage of Israel had joined with Absalom, but this Gentile warrior had chosen David.

David, who had been so full of words before, was suddenly quiet. He looked up at the Gentile with a look of appreciation and awe.

"What's your name, friend?"

"My name is Ittai, my lord."

"Go and pass over, Ittai. Go and pass over."

Chapter Twenty-Two

"For consider him that endured such contradiction of sinners against himself, lest ye be wearied and faint in your minds."
Hebrew 12:3

As David and his men journeyed, Joab fell back in the group to speak with Ittai. "I saw what happened back there and heard what you said to David. Do you know who I am, soldier?"

Ittai kept his eyes forward as he walked. "I know who you are."

"Good. Then you know I'm in charge of this army and that's not going to change."

"That's understood. I'm not looking to cause any problems."

Joab wasn't about to start trusting anyone, especially a Philistine. "Then why are you here? Why did you abandon your people?"

Ittai locked eyes with Joab for a moment, then he looked over at Abishai who was at the front of the column with David. "Because of him."

Joab lowered his voice. "Abishai? My brother? You left your people because of Abishai?"

"I never believed the legends until I saw it for myself," Ittai said. "Eleazar, Shammah, these men – what they've done, it's unnatural: killing hundreds of the enemy single-handedly. Then I saw Abishai do it. It was like there was something controlling him."

"It's called the anointing," Joab said. "You've heard of the stories of Samson, right? Our history records that the Holy Spirit would come upon him, and anoint him with power from on high."

Ittai interrupted. "Then he would slay a thousand of my people with a bone."

"Exactly."

The two walked in silence for a couple minutes, and then it was Ittai that spoke up again. "Your God is a God of war. My people cannot hope to stand up against him. I watched your brother kill three hundred of my men at Rephaim. My commanders refused to believe my report and I was scourged and exiled from my people. That is why I am here."

After a brief pause, Ittai spoke again. "Why are *you* here?

Joab was the type of man that always had an angle, and so he naturally assumed that everyone else did as well. However, this unpretentious man had disarmed the shyster. When presented with this question, Joab ignored his first reaction and decided to just take the question for what it was.

"I stay with David because I've seen what God does through him. I was too young to be at Elah, but I've seen him repeat it a dozen times over. I don't know how your people manage to breed such huge warriors, but I've seen David kill enough of them to know I need to stand behind the man and not against him."

At the front of the column there was a commotion. David put his hand up and swatted away a stone that was apparently thrown in his direction.

"Come on out, you bloody man! Flee! Run like the coward you are!"

A small, sickly looking man with wild eyes was running along the troop, cursing at David and casting dirt and stones in his direction.

"You filthy, treacherous Judean! The crown belongs to Benjamin, and you killed the king! You deserve it! You're a traitor! You've blood on your hands, son of Jesse! The LORD has rewarded you according to your works because you're a bloody man!"

No man talks to the king, any king, that way, Abishai thought as he turned to David. "Why should this dead dog curse my lord the king? Let me go over, I pray thee, and take off his head."

David closed his eyes and shook his head. "If I've said it once, I've said it hundred times— what have I to do with you, ye sons of Zeruiah? Let the man curse me. God told him to curse me."

David stopped and turned to face all the men that were following him. "My own son seeketh my life; what difference does it make that this Benjamite does as well? Leave him alone and let him curse me, for the LORD hath bidden him. Maybe the LORD will look upon my trouble and requite me good for his cursing this day."

When the procession went forward Ittai looked back to Joab. "No king on Earth would ever allow this. How does a man who could command so much fear willingly endure so much affliction?"

Joab smiled. "There's no king like David."

* * *

And while David and his band of men were journeying, another scene was transpiring within the city of Jerusalem. It certainly wasn't a procession of mourning as with David; it was all merriness and celebration in the City of Peace that day. It was a display of great pomp and gaudiness, for Absalom was his usual flamboyant self. The people were singing the praises of the new king as they lined the streets with palm leaves; men with trumpets led the way as a procession of dancers followed. There were horses and chariots and the riders threw trinkets and small treasures to the screaming crowd. And in the very middle of the whole thing was Absalom, the prince-turned-king, riding triumphantly upon a white horse and waving to the crowd.

Upon reaching the palace, Absalom majestically dismounted his steed and approached the steps where some nameless false prophet stood waiting before him. The man held his right hand up to silence the crowd and then began his speech, upon which Absalom immediately fell to one knee before the speaker. As the prophet spoke of the divine right and pedigree of the prince, he poured a few drops of oil upon his head and two other men placed a royal robe of purple and gold upon him. The crowd was breathless as the crown was placed upon his head, and he turned to face them.

Absalom's eyes seemed to glaze over for a few moments as he spoke. "I will sit upon the mount of the congregation, in the sides of the north: I will be like the most High."

And with that he ascended the steps of the palace and entered the throne room with all his company. All the normal people outside of the palace just looked at each other like a tree full of owls. "Well, he's certainly ambitious, isn't he?" one said to another.

Once entering the throne room Absalom quickly took the throne and smiled as he addressed his royal court. "Well, that was a lot easier than I thought it would be."

Everyone uproariously laughed of course, because that's just what you're supposed to do when the king tells a joke. All the lords and ladies were fawning over the new king, and the false prophet came and presented a golden scepter upon a scarlet covered pillow, which Absalom received thankfully.

One of the elders stepped forward. "The tribe of Ephraim pledges its support."

Then came another. "The tribe of Naphtali pledges its support."

And another. "The tribe of Judah pledges its support."

One by one they came, all pledging their allegiance to the new king. Absalom had not come in his father's name. He had come in his own name, and it was he whom they had received.

"All right, let's talk about our kingdom's primary threat right now."

"The Philistines?" one man asked.

Absalom laughed. "The Philistines? That scraggly bunch of cockroaches are holed up in Gath and are of no concern to me. We'll deal with them in time.

"My concern is David."

A hush fell over the room.

"Your Majesty," an elder said, "if you don't mind me saying so, why not leave well enough alone? David will just hide out in the wilderness as he did before."

Absalom nodded and looked down for a moment, and then stood to his full height and pointed his scepter at the man as his eyes flashed with rage. "Do I detect a hint of loyalty to the former regime? Do you seek a place among the rocks and caves of the Judean desert? Do not question my priorities again! Understood?"

"Yes, Lord Absalom. You are most merciful."

"Very well then; ideas anyone?"

Various ideas bounced around the room until Ahithophel spoke up. "My lord, David needs to be dealt with immediately. We must needs pursue him this night. Give me the honor of leading twelve thousand men after him. He'll be weak and worn out and I will smite the king only. The rest will naturally return peacefully, and you will have secured your kingdom."

"That's sounds like the best plan I've heard so far," Absalom said running his hand through his hair. "Simple and direct—"

Before he could finish the sentence, both doors of the palace opened. The sunlight painted the floor as the shadow from a dark silhouette entered the room. Squinting, people held their hands to their brows to see who it was. He was tall, lanky, and was wearing a flashy expensive robe. The guards to both sides of Absalom reached for their swords as the man approached.

The man stopped, pulled back his hood, and dramatically fell to one knee. "God save the king! God save the king!"

It was Hushai the Archite.

Absalom studied the man suspiciously. "Is this how you repay your friend? Is this your kindness unto him? Why didn't you leave with your friend?"

Hushai stood up and spoke. "Your Majesty, my service isn't limited to one man. I, like yourself, serve all of Israel."

Absalom was about to speak, but found that he couldn't really say anything to that. In a matter of seconds, Hushai had taken control of the floor. He continued to speak, this time addressing the entire room.

"When Absalom's father was king, I served him. Now that Absalom is king, I will serve him. All my life my desire has been to serve my people as a whole. My goal is the betterment of Israel. You all know me well."

At this point Hushai began to identify people by name, retelling old stories. The ambiance in the room became relaxed and lighthearted as people laughed, recalling fond memories.

"Very well then," Absalom said. "Do you have any advice for me at this time?"

"Yes I do," Hushai said, humbly of course.

"Well, go ahead."

"Thank-you, Your Majesty. The counsel of Ahithophel is not good at this time."

There was a small commotion that followed this, at which time Hushai held up his hands to quiet them. "This is nothing personal, of course! Ahithophel is a dear friend, why, our families have broken bread together many times."

There was something about the reference to Ahithophel's family that struck a nerve within him. He would have spoken up, but his conscience was killing him. His mind went to his granddaughter, Bathsheba, the real king's wife.

"In many situations it would be advisable to pursue the enemy while they appear to be tired, discouraged, and on the run. But my friends, this isn't just any foe we're facing here. This is David."

He paused for effect and looked around the room.

"This is David, and his Mighty Men."

And he paused again.

"Out there, right now, David has Benaiah. Beniah the giantkiller. Beniah the lionkiller! How many men have you known that have killed a lion?

"Oh, I know one," Hushai continued. "David! David killed a lion and a bear before he could even grow a beard! This is who we are talking about here.

"Shall I list off the accomplishments of the Mighty Men? Abishai, three hundred men single-handedly, with a spear. Jashobeam did the same thing. Then there's Adino, he killed eight hundred.

"Let's not forget that they're not alone. They also have six hundred mercenaries with them. All in all we're facing about a thousand men. We outnumber them twelve-to-one, but if their Mighty Men can kill hundreds in a single battle then twelve-to-one isn't good enough.

"While we may have thousands more in reserve, we can't afford to lose one battle. If we suffer a single defeat all the valiant men that remain will join with David and the kingdom will be lost."

Absalom stroked his beard. "Very well, Hushai, what do you suggest then?"

"For the glory of Israel and thy Majesty's sake, I suggest we gather a massive army from Dan even to Beersheeba. One that is as the sand of the sea for multitude!"

Hushai grew much more animated and dramatic at this point. "We shall cover him as the dew covereth the ground! There will be no place for him to hide. If he hide in a city, we will pull the entire city into the water and be rid of him! We shall amass an army so great that no group of Mighty Men could ever hope to stand against it. And you, my lord, shall lead them into victory."

The courtroom exploded in applause, and even Absalom himself stood. There were smiles all around as people gestured wildly and excitedly upon the new idea. It was an exciting idea to all of them, their brave new king leading a monolithic army out to crush the resistance. With all the frivolity that was ensuing, the only man who was still sitting was Ahithophel.

Ahithophel did not approve of the plan. He left the room quietly, rode his donkey back to his house, wrote a few letters to a few people, and then he simply put a rope around his neck and hung himself.

Hushai's plan seemed like such a good idea, but Ahithophel knew better.

Chapter Twenty-Three

"But whoso hath this world's good, and seeth his brother have need, and shutteth up his bowels *of compassion* from him, how dwelleth the love of God in him?"
I John 3:17

While Absalom was off garnering his tens of thousands of Hebrew soldiers to exterminate David, it was David that once again found himself sleeping under the stars. It was at this particular moment that he found that there was nothing he could do about his situation. Looking around, he saw that his men were exhausted. There were a few campfires, and the usual sentries moving about, but there was little conversation as most of the men were sound asleep by now.

David knew how the men felt; none of them wanted to flee. These were his mighty men, afraid of nothing. They followed their leader, frustrated, out to the wilderness. On top of the frustration and exhaustion they felt, they were hungry. The little food they had taken had been consumed, and there wasn't exactly any opportunities to hunt or gather while marching off into the desert.

David reached into his rucksack and brought out something with which to write. *LORD, how are they increased that trouble me! Many are they that rise up against me. Many there be which say of my soul, There is no help for him in God. Selah.*

David's mind went back to the days of flight under Saul. He remembered the nights under the sky back then, and the rest and protection the LORD had always given him. *But thou, O LORD, art a shield for me; my glory, and the lifter up of mine head. I cried unto the LORD with my voice, and he heard me out of his holy hill. Selah. I laid me down and slept; I awaked; for the LORD sustained me.*

The youngest son of Jesse, the boy of Judean hills, knew what was coming. His exhausted army was going to be hunted down by his own son and his own people. It was the ultimate betrayal and rejection. In spite of this, he wrote *I will not be afraid of ten thousands of people, that have set themselves against me round about.*

As David continued to write, one of his men came upon him so quickly it almost caught him off guard.

"Your Majesty! You're not going to believe this!" the man stammered.

David put his writing instrument down. "What is it?"

"There are three men here to see you, and they've brought—"

The young man was suddenly interrupted by a man old enough to be his grandfather. "Don't spoil the surprise for our nomadic and wandering king, young man."

David looked up to see Barzillai the Gileadite. The man was aged, but still retained his quick wit and charm. He was a man of great influence and wealth in his town. Smiling, Barzillai greeted David and helped himself to a rock upon which to sit. Two other men followed him, one a Gentile, but both remained standing.

Barzillai realized that he was sitting down and jumped back to his feet again. "Forgive me, David. Here are two friends of mine, Ammiel of Lodebar and Shobi, the son of Nahash the Ammonite."

David raised his eyebrows. "Hello Shobi, I knew your father. We both fled for our lives from the same man at different times. He helped me."

"It's a pleasure to meet you, King David," Shobi said. "My father spoke highly of you, which is why I am here,"

"Apparently not high enough! Your brother Hanun didn't exactly have your diplomatic grace."

"Yes, well, I am not my brother."

"Very well," David said. He turned to Ammiel, "And what brings you to my camp this night?"

Ammiel spoke to David. "Your Majesty, we have brought food and supplies for you and your men."

David looked over to the soldier that had brought him the news originally. "He speaks the truth," he said as his fished out a long list of items. "They have brought with them beds, basons, vessels, wheat, barley, flour, corn, beans, lentiles, pulse, honey, butter, sheep, cheese—"

David held his hand up. "Thank you, soldier. You are dismissed. Tell Abishai and Joab of this and have them distribute."

David smiled broadly. "I don't know how to thank you men for this; this is a little overwhelming to be honest."

Barzillai spoke. "You're a good man, David, and not all of Israel has sided with Absalom. I've watched you my whole life, and I'm not alone. There are many of us that are keeping to ourselves about the situation, but we want you back on the throne."

"I appreciate that, but it's in the LORD's hands."

Ammiel spoke up next. "Your Majesty, I come from Lodebar. I was there when the chariots arrived for Mephibosheth. That man was neglected and dirty; he was the offscouring of the town living by himself in a little shack. And yet you sent your messenger to come down and take him out of there. He didn't deserve that."

"No he didn't," David said. "I did it for Jonathan's sake. Jonathan earned it, and it was because of his righteousness that I saved Mephibosheth."

"Well," Ammiel continued, "I was there, and there were plenty of other people there as well that saw it. We support you, David. We love you and want you back on the throne. Any man who has the heart to do that, well, that's the man we want ruling Jerusalem."

And so it was that delightful evening that the stranger and the soldiers shared a meal and swapped stories. The loyal followers of God's anointed were blessed and refreshed by the kindness of three unexpected guests. One was an aged man who had seen David kill a giant and inspire an entire people that were at the present time very confused. Another was a man who refused to forget the past kindness of his newly scorned king.

Lastly, there was the son of an infamous Ammonite bandit who plagued Israel and threatened to destroy Jabesh-Gilead decades ago. David almost pondered the irony of the fact that he was running for his life from his own son, and yet the son of a villain had come to his aid.

But before he could consider this, David finished his
psalm.

*Salvation belongeth unto the LORD: thy blessing is upon
thy people. Selah.*

Chapter Twenty-Four

"So the people went out into the field against Israel: and the battle was in the wood of Ephraim;"
II Samuel 18:6

1023 B.C. The Woods of Ephraim

Months came and went as David and his men moved through the wilderness and woods, all the while staying one step ahead of Absalom. The rebel king's spies combed all of Israel searching for David and his sympathizers, and people saw quickly that the one whom they had received was not all he seemed to be. As Absalom's fist gripped tighter, more soldiers deserted him and joined David until his army grew to a little under ten thousand.

Finally the day had come and the real king of Israel stood before his woodland soldiers.

"I've assigned you men under the faithful leadership of Joab, Abishai, and Ittai. As you know, Absalom and his army will be upon us this day. The line will be drawn here, and the LORD will decide the fate of our land."

A few cheered and clapped, and then suddenly felt embarrassed because it was clear that David wasn't looking for that sort of response.

"The odds have been against us from the day we left Jerusalem. The LORD has sustained us by the charity of others and the provision of his wildlife. We have needed nothing during these months because it was the LORD who prepared us a table in the wilderness in the presence of our enemies.

"For those of you that fled with me under Saul this is nothing new to you, but what is different this time around is the number of others that have joined our ranks. We are not the same four hundred men that left that day."

David paused and looked sincerely at the men before him. "Thank-you for coming to our aid. I've been told that you refuse to have me out there with you. That's fine, so be it. I leave you with one final command, and it's the most important thing to remember today: spare my son, Absalom."

No one said anything, but no one liked the idea and David knew it.

"I understand he's the reason we're out here, and I know what he's done to our homes. But regardless he's my son, and I won't abide anyone killing my son. Is that understood?"

Everyone answered back in the affirmative.

"Very well then, you are dismissed. Let the LORD do what he will today."

*   *   *

By the tens of thousands they came through the woods of Ephraim. Absalom on his white horse flanked by Amasa, his general. They came on horses, mules and camels, with large groups of soldiers interspersed between cavalry units.

The vanguard unit ahead of Absalom and Amasa came to a halt as a young man ran up to them. "Oh, what's the matter now?" Absalom muttered as he watched the young man talking to the unit in front of him.

"General Amasa," one of the soldiers began, "the runner reports that our sentry units have encountered some action and that the road ahead is blocked."

"Finally!" Absalom interrupted.

Amasa was surprised to hear that. "Your Majesty, if you don't mind me saying so, but this has all the making of a trap. I recommend we hold up until we have more information."

"Oh forget all that! We have superior numbers; we can handle anything they'll throw at us. Send a detachment on ahead of us to clear the road and let's keep going."

"Very well," Amasa said and issued the order.

Suddenly an arrow struck Absalom's horse and he tumbled off as it reared. More arrows came from the woods on both sides of them and the men took cover behind logs and knolls and whatever else they could find. There was panic and confusion everywhere. Eight men came from the trees. Three of them led the way with a large net and the other five were providing cover-fire for the three. They threw a net over Absalom and started pulling him in the woods.

Amasa responded by rallying a band of Benjamites who succinctly overwhelmed the would-be kidnappers and recovered Absalom. "Get me another horse, now!" Absalom screamed as he threw the net off. A mule came running by and he pulled himself up onto it as it passed by.

Amasa was frustrated as the arrows kept coming down. "The king thinks he's invincible; ride with him! Protect him! Now!"

In all the confusion Amasa quickly realized there were now no horses to ride. Everyone had abandoned their mounts for cover. A captain at the rear attempted to dispatch a runner but the young man was shot down.

"Send more runners or we're finished!" Amasa called out. More runners fled, and more were cut down until a few made it through. Before Amasa could give an order for troop movement, the arrows stopped and there was silence. The attackers had left.

All over the woods of Ephraim the same hit-and-run attacks had been transpiring over and again. It seemed there was no rhyme or reason to it, but the men who fought for David were either legends or by now very used to woodland terrain and combat. This was second nature for the commanders who understood all to well that their greatest advantage lay in an unpredictable type of warfare.

Resting in their superior numbers, Absalom's men stormed into the woods to find their mysterious attackers. They slipped on the wet rocks, tripped over vines and holes in the ground, and easily became detached from their units. The battle was there scattered over the face of all the country, and the wood devoured more people that day than the sword devoured.

And then there was Absalom. As David's son he was naturally talented and dexterous when it came to battle. He also had the distinct advantage of being the one man on the battlefield that no one wanted to kill.

Well, almost no one.

He blazed aimlessly through the woods on his mule like a bandit, hacking down anyone who came near him. He jumped over logs and ducked branches, all the while evading capture. An arrow from behind him sliced through the air and grazed the side of his head. Absalom looked back just in time to see the bowmen nock another arrow. When he looked back in front of him, it was too late: a low hanging oak was upon him and when he ducked his hair, of all things, became entangled in the branches. Absalom screamed in pain as the mule kept running and left him hanging there by himself.

A few minutes later, Joab arrived with the bowman. "Why didn't you finish the job, soldier? I'd rewarded you personally if you had."

"There's no reward you could have given me to kill him, sir. I heard the king's command. We all heard it."

"I don't have time for this," Joab said and brushed the young man away. He stood before Absalom now.

"What. . . what are you doing?" Absalom winced in pain, pulling up on his hair to try and get some relief.

"Finishing the job," Joab said. "You had potential, boy, but you made your move too soon."

"Wait, I can make you my second in command, I can. . ."

"I save these for special occasions," Joab said as he revealed three six inch darts. "Considered yourself honored, or something like that."

And with that he pushed the darts into Absalom's heart and killed him.

Chapter Twenty-Five

"But the king covered his face, and the king cried with a loud voice, O my son Absalom, O Absalom, my son, my son!"
II Samuel 19:4

David waited in fearful anticipation as the runner tried to catch his breath. Another man had already delivered the news that the battle had been won, but David was concerned for his son.

"Well," David said impatiently, "What is the news?"

The man exhaled the words between gasps, "Tidings, my lord the king: for the LORD hath avenged thee this day of all them that rose up against thee."

"I know!" David said even more impatiently. "But what of the young man Absalom? Is the young man safe?"

Cushi, the runner, let out another breath and then said the words: "The enemies of my lord the king, and all that rise against thee to do thee hurt, be as that young man is."

It was with that news that the king's heart was shattered. He turned his back to his men and his cry shook the room. "Absalom, my son! Oh, my son Absalom! Would to God I had died for thee, O Absalom, my son, my son!"

David was completely consumed by his own grief and as such everyone quickly left the room. There was no one to solace him.

* * *

The journey back to Jerusalem was not a victorious welcome party. The soldiers and all those with them essentially had to sneak back in, all the while King David wept aloud for his son. The people loved David, and when David wept, they all wept right along with him.

Everyone except Joab, of course. At this moment he was entering into the house of the king. David sat in the shadows, his back to Joab.

"Your Majesty," Joab said, "You have shamed your people this day. They fought and bled on the battlefield for you. What about the lives of your soldiers, your wives and concubines, your sons and daughters? You've declared this day that you do not regard your princes nor servants. If Absalom had lived and we had all died, would that have made you happy?"

With a roar David spun off the chair, grabbed Joab and threw him on the table. Joab tried to get up but David smote his face and held him back down. Before he could respond, David pulled Joab's own dagger from his belt and put it to the general's throat.

"You're a murderer, Joab." David hissed in fury. "You deserve to die. You killed my son."

Joab's face showed no fear, but he was struggling to breath and choked out the words. "Have you forgotten that it was your son that killed your son? Have you forgotten that we all deserved to die? Did you forget that I brought Absalom to you to begin with? I never wanted this. "

David gritted his teeth and let him go. Joab crawled off the table and naturally distanced himself from the king. "David, he would have just started another rebellion. We were on the battlefield; things happen. My brother died on the battlefield."

David didn't respond.

Joab let out a sigh. "King, those men out there just won back your kingdom for you. Every last one of them would lay down his life for you. They don't care that Absalom was your son; to them he was the man who wanted you dead.

"Now there's nothing but discouragement and confusion in this whole city. They don't know what to think. If you don't go out there and be the leader you are, then someone else is going to take your place again. Speak comfortably unto your people, or you're going to lose them."

And with that, the general left David alone.

* * *

The king went before his people that fitful evening and thanked them for their courage and for saving the kingdom. His heart was all over the place. All he really cared about was the loss of his son, but he knew that Joab was right. The people deserved his thanks and so he swallowed his feelings and did what was right by his people.

On the other hand, David's guilty conscience prevented him from enacting justice upon Joab that night. He would soon regret his hesitation because it wasn't long before Joab murdered another man: Amasa, Absalom's former general. David had tried to pull the rug out from under Joab by replacing him as military leader with Amasa. Joab wouldn't stand for it and killed him. Once again, David refused to deal with Joab because of his own guilt and because of Joab's popularity. Around and around they went for years and years.

David was a man of war, but he failed to go to battle and got caught up with Bathsheba that terrible night. Moreover he also failed to go to battle the day that Absalom was killed. He learned from that and from thereon despite the insistence of his men, he went out to fight with them time and time again.

There was the time in which David, as an old man, faced a giant alone on the battlefield. He had slain many giants before and so mentally he was prepared. He anticipated every lumbering and crashing move the behemoth would make, but David's body wasn't as sharp as his mind was. His strength failed him, and he wasn't as quick as he used to be. Fortunately, Abishai saved his life that day and slew the giant. After that, the consensus of the men was clear: "Thou shalt go no more out with us to battle, that thou quench not the light of Israel."

Joab, for all his problems, kept the kingdom in check along with his brother Abishai. The kingdom spread and any uprising was smashed before it could grow. As for David, he spent the twilight of his life gathering materials for the temple his son would one day build.

Chapter Twenty-Six

"He shall have dominion also from sea to sea, and from the river unto the ends of the earth."
Psalm 72:8

1015 B.C. Jerusalem

The aged king lay on his bed speaking as his son Solomon sat next to him listening. The shepherd boy's face was now old and scarred from warfare. His voice was still strong, but he was hard of hearing now— the chaos and roar of the battlefield having taken its toll. David's mind was sharp up to the very end, but his body gave out on him. He was too thin; he had a hard time staying warm.

"Son," David would say in the many talks he had with Solomon, "listen to me, son. If thou wilt receive my words, and hide my commandments with thee, so that thou incline thine ear unto wisdom, and apply thine heart to understanding, then shalt thou understand the fear of the LORD, and find the knowledge of God."

"Father, so much of the time you speak in dark sayings, but I'm trying to understand," Solomon said.

"You're doing just fine, son. A young man will hear, and will increase learning. A man of understanding shall attain unto wise counsels."

"Beware of the strange woman. For by means of a whorish woman a man is brought to a piece of bread: and the adulteress will hunt for the precious life."

Solomon listened intently, but David could see something bothered him.

"Son," David said. "Your mother and I made a terrible mistake. No, it wasn't a mistake; it was sin. A lot of people died because of what we did. God said four lambs; I lost three sons and a nephew. I spent the rest of my life fighting because of that sin."

"But you and mother were forgiven?"

"Yes, God was merciful to us. He forgave us for what we had done, and he used us, but we both lost a piece of our hearts and a piece of that joy we used to have. Nothing was ever the same. Grace is always greater than sin, but a man reaps what he sows."

Solomon looked intently at his father.

"Listen to me, son. There are places you should never go and things you should never do. Don't let the natural curiosity inside of you get the best of you."

"Yes, Father."

"You're going to have to clean up some of my messes when you become king, boy. You're going to have to deal with Joab. He's a murderer, and God's word says to take no satisfaction for the life of a murderer. He was also behind that attempted coup to get Adonijah to be anointed instead of you. Finish him off son; he'll be nothing but trouble for you. There are others you'll have to take care of as well. We'll talk about them another time."

Long into the night the conversations went like this. David was passing down wisdom to his son. "Boast not thyself of tomorrow," he'd say. "A good name is rather to be chosen than great riches." "It is not for kings, my son, it is not for kings to drink wine."

"There are four types of people in the world, son. First off, there's the scorner. He's only out to cause trouble. You can't try to straighten him out. He that reproveth a scorner getteth to himself shame, but many times you have to. Understand this: when the scorner is punished, the simple is made wise.

"And then there's the simple. When it comes to the simple, they'll usually believe and follow whoever gets to them first. The simple believeth every word, but the prudent man looketh well to his going. The adversary will devour the simple with half-truths. He'll emphasis things without telling the full story; and by the misplaced virtue of the simple, he'll cause havoc.

"The fool is different from both of them. The scorner is about pride, deception and destruction – but the fool couldn't care less. He has no loyalty and just gives into whatever feels best and is easiest. It's all about fun for the fool. A foolish son is a grief to his father, and bitterness to her that bare him. Don't waste your life with the fool. Forsake the foolish, and live; and go in the way of understanding.

"Lastly, son, there's the wise man. A wise man will hear, and will increase learning. A wise man stays away from sin. In fact, you can rebuke a wise man, and he'll love you for rebuking him. A wise man feareth, and departeth from evil: but the fool rageth, and is confident. A wise son maketh a glad father: but a foolish man despiseth his mother."

David poured his heart, his life, his entire being into Solomon. He loved his son and wanted him to do better than he had done.

There was one particular night in which David read to Solomon a special psalm he had written expressly for him.

"Son, you asked me what kept me going all those days of turmoil and war. I'm going to tell you what it was, and why I didn't go insane with all the warfare as Saul did. I wrote you a psalm, and I'd like to read a few portions of it to you to answer that question.

"Give the king thy judgments, O God, and thy righteousness unto the king's son. He shall judge thy people with righteousness, and thy poor with judgment. The mountains shall bring peace to the people, and the little hills, by righteousness. He shall judge the poor of the people; he shall save the children of the needy, and shall break in pieces the oppressor. They shall fear thee as long as the sun and moon endure, throughout all generations.

"You know who I'm talking about, right, son?"

"The Messiah." Solomon said.

"That's right. In the end, it's all about him. One day he's coming back to fix this mess. That's what it's all about, son."

Solomon nodded. "I'd like to hear more, if that's all right, Father."

"In his days shall the righteous flourish; and abundance of peace so long as the moon endureth," David said. "He shall have dominion also from sea to sea, and from the river unto the ends of the earth. They that dwell in the wilderness shall bow before him; and his enemies shall lick the dust.

"Yea, all kings shall fall down before him: all nations shall serve him.

"For he shall deliver the needy when he crieth; the poor also, and him that hath no helper. He shall spare the poor and needy, and shall save the souls of the needy. He shall redeem their soul from deceit and violence: and precious shall their blood be in his sight."

Solomon could feel a tear forming as his father read the psalm. He understood clearly that this was his father's heart and passion. It was the LORD. In spite of David's mistakes, and in spite of the trouble he had with his spirit at times, he had a deep love for the LORD, maybe more than any man who ever lived. Solomon knew that the greatness of his father wasn't in his sword, his leadership, or his ability to inspire men. The greatness of his father was in his heart. It wasn't *limited* to loyalty to the LORD. David wasn't simply dedicated to God; his primary delight, passion and hunger *was* in God. His heart was after God's own heart.

"His name shall endure for ever: his name shall be continued as long as the sun: and men shall be blessed in him: all nations shall call him blessed," David said.

"Blessed be the LORD God, the God of Israel, who only doeth wondrous things. And blessed be his glorious name for ever: and let the whole earth be filled with his glory; Amen, and Amen."

The prayers of David the son of Jesse are ended.

Chapter Twenty-Seven

"Take heed to thyself that thou offer not thy burnt
offerings in every place that thou seest:
But in the place which the LORD shall choose in one of
thy tribes, there thou shalt offer thy burnt offerings,
and there thou shalt do all that I command thee."
Deuteronomy 12:13-14

1014 B.C. Jerusalem

The sweet psalmist of Israel, the man after
God's own heart, David, had died. Now
Solomon was king. Solomon had a calming
influence upon the kingdom. While David was king,
things were constantly up and down. The people loved
and admired David, and most knew he was a hero the
likes of which Israel hadn't seen in a long time, but the
times of David were turbulent times.

The new king bided his time, but didn't hesitate in
carrying out David's instructions when the opportunities
availed themselves. Shimei, a troublemaker, essentially
violated his probation and was executed by Beniah for
doing so. There was Adonijah who was executed as well
for attempting to start a second coup.

And of course, there was Joab. The self-serving,
murderous politician-soldier who turned against
Solomon at the end of David's life; he too was executed.
Solomon gave the order to Benaiah to kill Joab because
he had murdered Amasa and Abner. Benaiah couldn't

help but wonder why Absalom's death wasn't listed in
the charges against Joab, but he didn't ask.

It was a sad and pitiful thing, and like Joab's life, it
was a mixture of regret and respect. Joab fled to the
tabernacle, sword in hand, while everyone who saw him
scrambled out of his way.

I've got to grab the horns! Joab thought to himself. *I
have to die holy, if it's the one thing I do, I have to die holy!*

Upon reaching the gate, Joab looked inside. The
priests looked back at him, and backed away from the
brazen laver. Panting and sweating, his eyes darting
back and forth like he was still on the battlefield, the old
warrior dropped his sword and ran to the altar. He fell
before it and grabbed the horns.

"God! You said whatever touches the horns is holy!"
He cried aloud, "Make me holy before I die! Forgive me,
oh God. Forgive me!"

"Joab," a voice said behind him, "You need to come
over here."

Joab wiped the sweat from his eyes and looked
behind him. It was Benaiah, sword in hand. His face
was set like a flint, he had a duty to perform, but Joab
could see right through him.

"I'm not leaving this altar, Benaiah. If you're going
to kill me, you need to do it here."

Unsure of what to do, Benaiah reported back to
Solomon who simply told him to kill Joab where he
stood, and then to bury him. It needed to end. So
Benaiah returned and stood at the doorway yet again,
and saw Joab in the same spot he had left him at before.

Benaiah was a huge man and not intimidated by anyone on the battlefield. He had slain a lion and several giants. He was more than a match for Joab, and Joab knew it. Benaiah's chest heaved as he breathed; he was nervous. This was different.

"C'mon, soldier, do your duty!" Joab barked at Benaiah.

"Joab, I just want you to know that —"

"Oh mush!" Joab said. "You're not telling me anything I don't already know. Let's just get this over with. Get over here and give me a soldier's death. I got it coming. I deserve it."

Joab, old and gray, slowly stood to his full height. His eyes narrowed in the bright sunlight as Benaiah approached. Joab never winced or even closed his eyes as Benaiah raised his sword in the air. As the blade came down, the old general just looked his fellow soldier in the eye.

And he never let go of the horns of that altar.

* * *

Solomon was relatively young, and he knew that. He rightly felt overburdened with the responsibility that lay upon his shoulders. He knew he was blessed beyond measure, and considered many times that it was around his age his father was running for his life from Saul or facing Philistine giants on the battlefield. Things had really changed. He was facing down angry politicians and foreign heads of state that didn't like his policies. Sometimes he'd prefer the giants.

In the process of time Solomon married the daughter of Pharaoh, thinking it to be the diplomatic way to secure the southern region. Of course in doing so Solomon had ignored the scripture that commanded the people not to intermarry with the heathens of the land.

The people and Solomon had been sacrificing unto the LORD in the high mountainous places. These were the places that the former nations had worshipped their gods by offering human sacrifices, sending their children through the fire, and prostituting their daughters. Because of this, God had strictly commanded the people under Moses to not mix his worship with the pagan worship – even when it came down to the location of worship. The excuse of course was that there wasn't a temple built yet, but in the back of everyone's minds they all knew that regardless of the excuse they were supposed to be sacrificing their sin offerings in Jerusalem. A few people thought about saying something about the subtle seeds of apostasy that were apparent, but they decided the charitable and gracious thing to do was to mind their own business.

Though there was clear compromise, Solomon still loved the LORD, and on one day alone he sacrificed over a thousand burnt offerings in Gibeon. Though the sacrifice was done in the wrong place, the LORD was merciful to Solomon and appeared to him in the middle of the night in a dream.

"Ask what I shall give thee," the LORD said.

With the weight of government upon him, it was the perfect time for the question, so in his dream Solomon spoke from his heart. "You showed an immense amount of mercy to my father David, as he walked before you in truth and righteousness.

"And LORD, I'm not anything like my father. I'm a little child; I know not how to go out or come in. This is such a tremendous burden that is upon me, you have such a great people that cannot be numbered! Please give me a heart of understanding to judge thy people that I may discern between the good and the bad. Who, LORD, is able to judge this thy so great a people?"

The request touched the heart of God, and he granted Solomon his desire. God told Solomon that he was going to give him a wise and understanding heart like none before or after him, and that he was going to grant him riches and honor unlike any of the other kings of his day.

When Solomon awoke the next morning he offered a sacrifice unto the LORD, only this time he offered it in Jerusalem.

Chapter Twenty-Eight

"So that the priests could not stand to minister because of the cloud: for the glory of the LORD had filled the house of the LORD."
I Kings 8:11

1004 B.C. Jerusalem

The kingdom was established in the hand of Solomon, the son of David, the son of Jesse. Solomon desired peace and began negotiations with the nations around him. One by one they all would become tributaries to Solomon. They understood clearly the might of Israel and thought it best to take the offers that were given them. Gold and silver, spices and fruits, livestock, building supplies – it all poured into Israel.

It was in the fourth year of his reign that Solomon began the construction of the temple, and he threw himself wholly into the project. Solomon spared no expense in acquiring massive amounts of stone, wood, gold, brass, iron, marble, granite— the list went on and on as he placed his people under hard labor and taxation to gather and build. The cedar and fir trees of Lebanon floated down the great sea to Joppa, from which they were hauled to Jerusalem. Year after year the people labored to build the house of the LORD.

After seven years the project was complete, and what a beautiful sight it was. Gone were the days of the tent in the wilderness, because the walls around the temple were now made of stone. It was the architectural wonder of the world and the most glorious building on the face of the earth. All the while it had been built there was never the sound of an axe or any tool, for the materials were prepared ready to fit into place. The entire inside of the temple was overlaid with gold and had carvings of palm trees and cherubims and open flowers. The value and cost of the solid gold, silver and brass contents within the temple would bankrupt many nations, let alone the cost of the temple itself. There was truly a diamond in Jerusalem, all to the glory of Jehovah.

The day for the dedication of the temple had finally come. The Ark of the Covenant was carried by the priests into the Holy of Holies as sheep and oxen without number were being sacrificed and offered unto the LORD. As soon as the ark was put in its place and the priests stepped into the courtyard, a holy cloud of Shekinah glory filled the temple.

A hush fell over the crowd when they saw the cloud of the LORD's glory. Solemnly, they turned to Solomon who was about to speak.

"The LORD said that he would dwell in the thick darkness."

Solomon bowed his head and held his hands to the skies. "I have surely built thee an house to dwell in, a settled place for thee to abide in for ever."

Turning again to the congregation Solomon continued. "Blessed be the LORD God of Israel, which spake with his mouth unto David my father, and hath with his hand fulfilled it, saying, Since the day that I brought forth my people Israel out of Egypt, I chose no city out of all the tribes of Israel to build an house, that my name might be therein; but I chose David to be over my people Israel.

"And it was in the heart of David my father to build an house for the name of the LORD God of Israel."

Solomon spoke of his father who was a man of war and that the LORD had forbidden him to build the temple. It was the son of David that was to accomplish the great vision of his father.

"I am risen up in the room of David my father, and sit on the throne of Israel, as the LORD promised, and have built an house for the name of the LORD God of Israel."

It was at this time that Solomon began to pray. His eyes were closed as he spoke and both of his hands were spread forth toward heaven.

"LORD God of Israel, there is no God like thee, in heaven above, or on earth beneath."

As he continued he fell to his knees as well as did all the people of Israel. "But will God indeed dwell on the earth? Behold, the heaven and heaven of heavens cannot contain thee; how much less this house that I have builded? This house is yours LORD; it is the best we can offer.

"O LORD God, please hearken unto the voice of thy people when they pray to this place. May your eyes be open to this house night and day, even toward the place of which thou hast said, my name shall be there.

"Father, when your people are smitten before thee, may they pray to you in this place. When they sin, may they turn to you in this place. When the heaven is shut up and there is no rain, may they pray to this place and confess thy name and turn from their sin. O God, please hear their prayer and forgive them.

"If the stranger from another nation prays unto this place, hear thou in heaven.

"LORD, if thy people go to battle against an enemy, please hear their prayer.

"LORD, if thy people sin against thee, and are carried away captive unto the land of the enemy, far or near, and they repent and pray unto thee. Should they return unto thee with all their heart, and all their soul, and cry unto this city and this place and this house; please hear from heaven and forgive their sin and heal their land.

"We be thy people, O LORD God, the people thou brought out of the furnaces of Egypt. We are thine inheritance that thou didst separate from among all the people of the earth."

After this Solomon stood and blessed the congregation with a loud voice saying, "Blessed be the LORD, that hath given rest unto his people Israel, according to all that he promised: there hath not failed one word of all his good promise, which he promised by the hand of Moses his servant.

"The LORD our God be with us, as he was with our fathers: let him not leave us, nor forsake us:

"That he may incline our hearts unto him, to walk in all his ways, and to keep his commandments, and his statutes, and his judgments, which he commanded our fathers.

"And let these my words, wherewith I have made supplication before the LORD, be nigh unto the LORD our God day and night, that he maintain the cause of his servant, and the cause of his people Israel at all times, as the matter shall require:

"That all the people of the earth may know that the LORD is God, and that there is none else.

"Let your heart therefore be perfect with the LORD our God, to walk in his statutes, and to keep his commandments, as at this day."

The people shouted and cried unto the LORD in a chorus of worship and the sound of praise filled the air. Those within the third Heaven watched in amazement as the people celebrated the LORD and offered thousands of sacrifices unto him. It was something that had never been seen before or done before; the focus of the entire universe was upon the temple at Mount Zion.

"LORD," Gabriel said to God, "Surely you'll send them the seed now? It's what David wanted; it's what all the ancients wanted. They're altogether in the land and the temple is built."

"No, Gabriel, not yet. They still have that sin problem, and there will be no kingdom until that sin has been dealt with."

"But LORD, I don't understand. They're offering the sacrifices right now. That's what you said it takes to have the sins forgiven. If they're ever clean enough and forgiven enough, wouldn't it be right now?"

"None of those are perfect, Gabriel. It will take the perfect sacrifice to take away their sins. They have a long way to go, but one day the sun of righteousness will arise with healing in his wings. It will be the Lamb of God that will take away the sins of the world."

Gabriel didn't say anything else; he just thought. His mind raced back to Eden and the animal skins. He thought further of Abraham's words on the mount. He thought of the Passover and how the LORD had said that the whole assembly of the congregation would be guilty of killing the male lamb; the male lamb that was without blemish and without spot.

"The lamb of God," Gabriel said to himself. "The lamb of God."

Chapter Twenty-Nine

"Remove not the ancient landmark, which thy fathers have set."
Proverbs 22:28

1004 B.C. Jerusalem

It wasn't many days after the dedication and celebration of the temple that the LORD appeared again unto Solomon in another dream.

"Solomon, I have heard your prayer and supplication that you made before me, and I have hallowed this house to put my name there forever. My eyes will always be upon Mount Zion and my heart will always be upon Jerusalem.

"And if thou wilt walk before me as David thy father did, with all of thine heart, then I will establish your kingdom forever. If you will walk with me in the uprightness of thine heart then I will establish the kingdom and throne of Solomon forever.

"But if not, Solomon, if you turn from following me or your children turn from following me, then I will cut off Israel from the land that I've given them. Israel shall be cast out of my sight and all those that pass by shall ask why I have done this."

Solomon sat up in his bed in a cold sweat. The room was dark and he was alone. The king knew his position was conditional upon obedience, but being reminded of it again was nerve-racking.

He slipped to his knees by his bed. "LORD, I'm trying. These people, these other nations— I have to work with them. I have to negotiate and be diplomatic. I want to be a man of peace, and sometimes that means compromise. It's give and take. God have mercy on me and my people. LORD help me.

"LORD? Are you there LORD?"

But the LORD wasn't there. Everything that needed to be said to Solomon had already been said by God. Someone else was in the room with him though, and that person was none other than the fifth cherub, the prince of darkness grim, Satan. He couldn't read Solomon's mind, so he hadn't seen the dream – but he saw Solomon's reaction and heard his words he prayed back to God. And as Solomon wept and prayed to the LORD, Satan got on his knees right next to the conflicted king and put his arm around him and whispered to him.

* * *

Time passed and things changed in Israel. It was as if the constant peace over time took something out of the people. They didn't have anything to fight about and they became lackluster in their souls. The constant hard labor took the men out of their homes for long periods of time. It was hard to tell what was happening in Israel, but the people as a whole were becoming hollow and there was a certain inward decay and sadness in the air.

Solomon wasn't anything like his father, and it was a disappointment to the people. The man wore several different hats: he was a king, a debater, a scientist, a philosopher, a writer, and an architect. He taxed and worked the people for his massive building projects and social programs. He wrote great works of wisdom that through the coming ages other men would attempt to repackage and claim as their own. He studied all manners of trees, rivers, wildlife, and cultures. He threw himself wholly into every project, idea, or research he could find.

Though he was brilliant, there was something wrong with Solomon's heart. You would have never seen

Solomon running down the streets of Jerusalem dancing before the ark in a shepherd's skirt like David his father. You'd never see Solomon out on the hills by himself singing and making music to the LORD. One would never dare to say that Solomon didn't love the LORD, but he didn't have the heart of his father.

Eventually Solomon's curiosity led him to places he should have never gone. He would experiment with things he had no business toying with. He would drink himself drunk just to see what it was like and document the experience. He toyed around with black magic and the dark side of the spirit world. His wives led him to places he never thought he'd ever go. At first, much of this was done in private, but like anything it would eventually come out publically.

But way before Solomon went down that road, a preacher man came to him. It was probably on a busy day for Solomon and probably at the most inopportune time. It was probably on a day just like the day that Nathan confronted David.

"Your Majesty!" Ahijah the prophet said bowing before the king who was on his throne.

"Make it short, I haven't a lot of time these days," Solomon said as he peered over the top of a book. It was the third one he'd read that day. He simply devoured them and tossed them away like an apple core.

"Your Majesty, I have a word from the LORD for you today," Ahijah began.

"Now wait just a minute there," Solomon said, putting his book aside. "You prophets are just so dogmatic at times. How do you know it was from the

LORD? How do you know it wasn't just some kind of impression you had at the time? You do realize of course that the basis of the message that you're about to lay upon me is subject to multiple interpretations, right? Why, you can get ten people in the same room and they can all look at it and come up with ten different conclusions! Who's to say that your conclusion is the right one?"

Ahijah wasn't rattled, of course; he was a seasoned prophet and understood that his job wasn't to convince the king, or frankly anyone else, of anything. Any prophet worth his salt knew his job was just to deliver the message and let whatever followed just happen.

He began again. "Your Majesty! Thus saith the LORD: quit your compromisin' or your gonna live to regret it!"

Solomon chuckled. He had a bona fide, genuine, in-the-flesh hayseed preacher in front of him. Why, didn't he realize that his ways were old fashioned? Didn't this old man understand that if God was going to speak to Solomon through a preacher he would use a man of high intellectual degree, couth, and someone who could at least speak without using crude contractions and colloquialisms?

"I hardly think," Solomon said with a smile, "that the LORD put it quite that way."

"The LORD gives us prophets a little liberty in our delivery, king. You'd know that if'n you were right with God!"

Solomon was a little irritated at that remark. "And just how do you know if I'm right with God or not? You don't know my heart! Why, I'm very sincere in how I live my life and-"

"Beggin' your pardon, Your Majesty, but your heart has nothing to do with it. Anyone with a lick o' sense can see what you're doin' jus ain't right!"

The red-faced king leaned forward in his throne. "You know what you are? You're nothing more than a judgmental Pharisee!"

The prophet just looked at Solomon with a strange and confused look. "What's a Pharisee?"

Solomon coughed and sat back. "Well, it's a . . . hmmm . . . it just seemed like the thing to say at the time, that's all."

"King," Ahijah began again, "You've done some wonderful things for the LORD. But you've opened the floodgates of paganism into our land and you and our nation are backsliding."

"What's wrong with a little diversity?" Solomon said.

The prophet wouldn't bite on the attempt to redefine a term. "Paganism, Your Majesty, is the worship of devils and false gods. You're letting your people worship Jehovah and Satan at the same time, and while Satan doesn't mind that, the LORD has a big problem with it!"

Solomon squeezed his forehead and let out a sigh. "How am I mixing paganism with the worship of Jehovah?"

"The people are offering sacrifices on the high places."

"What's wrong with that? They're offering sacrifices to Jehovah! If someone wants to worship God out on the mountains instead of in the temple who am I to argue with that?"

"The Scriptures say those sacrifices are to be offered only in Jerusalem!"

"Oh, you're such a literalist!" Solomon replied.

"And the music," the prophet said with his finger pointing at the king, "that music is from the pit of Hell! That pagan sex music was used in their worship services as they fornicated and sacrificed their children! It has no business being anywhere near our people!"

"Well," Solomon said, "they changed the words, and music is neutral. It's really all about the heart of worship and ushering someone into the presence of—"

"Notes," the prophet's face was red and his voice was booming now, "are neutral, Your Majesty. Lines on a wall are neutral, Your Majesty. Letters on a page are neutral. But you get enough o' those things together and you make a message!

"Lines make pictures – and our God told us to destroy their pictures when we entered the land!

"Letters make words – words that communicate a message, and not all messages are neutral, Your Majesty!

"Notes make music – and anyone with any lick 'o sense knows that music is a language that everyone understands! You're letting your people use music that has been generationally used to propel fornication, drunkenness, violence, and Satanism!"

The king just looked at the man and scowled. "Well, I don't want to be judgmental and alienate anyone. Jehovah is for all you know."

"King," the backwoods prophet's voice was much calmer now, "the only way to be non-judgmental to everyone in this world is to not draw a line on anything at all. If you're not going to draw a line on marrying heathen women, or disobeying the law in sacrifices, or mixing paganism in your music – then where in the world are ya gonna draw a line?"

He continued. "You listen to me now. I've already argued with you long enough on this. The message from the LORD is plain and simple and you can take it however you want. You and your kinfolk are the ones who are gonna have to deal with the consequences if you try to fool yourself into thinkin' that what you've been up to is okay!

"You keep down this road and the day will come when you're worshiping the pagan gods yourself and God's going to rip the kingdom from you just like he did from Saul!"

The king stood up in a rage. "Get out! Get out! Get out of my throne room now! Get out!"

The prophet left with a broken heart, but the message had been delivered.

Chapter Thirty

"Of which salvation the prophets have enquired and searched diligently, who prophesied of the grace *that should come* unto you:"
I Peter 1:10

978 B.C. Jerusalem

The prophet was right and the king never stopped from his path of darkness until the very twilight of his life. His wives had drawn his heart away from the LORD unto the gods and practices of paganism. Solomon repented towards the end of his life and declared all things as vanity. He came to a point where he had a greater appreciation for the simpler things, as the old prophet would put them, and declared for all to *fear God, and keep his commandments: for this is the whole duty of man.*

At some point a man arose in the kingdom, a very industrious man who was also a man of valour by the name of Jeroboam. Jeroboam had a good head on his shoulders and Solomon gave him a good deal of authority. But, as the providence of God would have it, there were a lot of tremors in the kingdom at the time. More and more people were speaking out against the king and his practices, be it religious or governmental; and Jeroboam wound up being one of them. Solomon dispatched an assassin to deal with Jeroboam, but the wily man had his ear to the ground and was making preparations to escape to Egypt.

I've got to get out of here, Jeroboam thought as he paid the woman. He grabbed the fruits, put them in his sack, and stole a quick glance over his shoulder. The man with the hood was still there, standing in the shadows, dark and grim.

Jeroboam thanked the woman and walked away as quickly and discreetly as he could. He left the Jerusalem market and began to walk through the residential districts of the city, all the while trying to shake the dark stranger that followed. Jeroboam slid into a dark corner, grabbed a new garment he had bought, and slipped it on over what he was wearing. *I'll lose him now,* he thought.

When he stepped back into the narrow alley, he looked both ways. The stranger was gone. Jeroboam heaved a sigh of relief and walked out into an open area that was the beginning of some farmland. Jeroboam took about ten steps and then an icy chill suddenly came over him. He had the overwhelming feeling that he was not alone, and he was terrified to turn around.

And so he didn't. He just stood there, transfixed in his spot. A most unusual thing happened next: there was no knife to the back, no rag held to his face, not even a solid thump on the head. Instead, Jeroboam felt a tug, followed by the long and irritating sound made when material tears.

He spun around half-expecting to see a child, but instead it was the mysterious hooded stranger. Jeroboam was speechless. The hooded man reached for his throat, and grabbed his collar and ripped it off. Jeroboam blinked, and the man grabbed his sleeve and tore it off.

"What are you doing?" Jeroboam said in mixture of terror and astonishment.

"Jus never you mind, fancy-pants," the hooded man said and ripped off another piece.

"Never me mind? You're ripping my brand new clothes!"

"Take it up with God, boy! I'm jus doing what he told me to!" the stranger said. His hood fell back and Jeroboam finally saw who it was: Ahijah the prophet.

"What, what, what are you ripping my clothes up for?" Jeroboam stammered.

"It's a picture o' something, son. That and I think God gets a kick out of makin' his prophets do stuff like this," Ahijah said as he ripped the last piece off. He looked up at Jeroboam, who stood there in tattered rags with his mouth wide open.

"Better close yer mouth, sonny, before a fly lands in it."

Jeroboam paused, and then scowled at the prophet. "Now what?"

"Now, you grab ten of those and put them back into your bag, that's what."

Jeroboam did as he was told.

"Good," Ahijah said, "I'm not sure what would have happened if you had argued with me. Don't argue with a prophet, son. If there's anything you should know, it's don't argue with a prophet."

"Yes sir," Jeroboam said as he took off his hat.

Ahijah rolled his shoulders and raised his right hand in the traditional manner in which a prophet did when he delivered a message. "Thus saith the LORD, the God of Israel, Behold, I will rend the kingdom out of the hand of Solomon, and will give ten tribes to thee:

"Because that they have forsaken me, and have worshipped Ashtoreth the goddess of the Zidonians, Chemosh the god of the Moabites, and Milcom the god of the children of Ammon, and have not walked in my ways, to do that which is right in mine eyes, and to keep my statutes and my judgments, as did David his father.

"Howbeit I will not take the whole kingdom out of his hand: but I will make him prince all the days of his life for David my servant's sake, whom I chose, because he kept my commandments and my statutes:

"But I will take the kingdom out of his son's hand, and will give it unto thee, even ten tribes."

I'm not that ambitious! Jeroboam thought.

The prophet continued speaking. "And it shall be, if thou wilt hearken unto all that I command thee, and wilt walk in my ways, and do that is right in my sight, to keep my statutes and my commandments, as David my servant did; that I will be with thee, and build thee a sure house, as I built for David, and will give Israel unto thee."

That was the end of the message, and so the prophet stopped talking. Jeroboam looked up at him. "Thanks, I appreciate that, but I'm not interested in the job. With royalty usually comes a lot of other trouble that I'd rather avoid."

The prophet smiled. "You're right about that, sonny. Being a prophet of the LORD ain't that much different I reckon. But we ain't got much choice in the matter. If

God gives you a job to do, you gotta do it. You understand?"

"I suppose so."

"Listen, boy. You have an amazing opportunity here!" Ahijah said thumping his finger on the man's chest. "If you follow the LORD and obey his commands, you'll get in on that Abrahamic promise! Why, that promise went from the garden over to Abraham and then to Moses, Joshua and David. God is so fed up with David's kinfolk that he's going to let you in this promise! He's giving you ten tribes! You stay right, and if your kinfolk stay right, then when the kingdom finally does come, your name will be just as great as David's if not greater! Your line will have ten tribes in the final kingdom and his will only have two!"

"Wow," Jeroboam said. "I guess I never even considered that. Does that mean God changed his mind or something? God's not breaking his promise, is he?"

"Of course not! The promise is that all this land is going to belong to Abraham's boys. The deceiver will be walloped, and the promised seed will be here to do whatever it is that he's going to do that's so great!"

"What is it he's going to do?"

Ahijah lowered his head. "That's a good question, and you'd think I'd know the answer. My prophet friends and myself have enquired and searched diligently on that matter, and, frankly, we're a little confused. Sometimes the scriptures speak of him ruling and reigning, and other times it talks about him suffering and dying."

"Hmm." Jeroboam said.

"Hmm is right," Ahijah replied.

"I like the part about him ruling and reigning best."

"Yeah, me too. We try just to focus on that part."

Chapter Thirty-One

"With the ancient *is* wisdom; and in length of days understanding."
Job 12:12

975 B.C. Jerusalem

Toward the end of his life, Solomon did repent and saw the vanity of a life outside of God's will. In the final years he made attempts to pass these things on to his son Rehoboam. "My son, attend unto my wisdom," he would say. "My son, forget not my law," or "My son, keep thy father's commandment." Over and over again he admonished his son to love wisdom and seek after understanding.

But eventually Solomon died, and the time came for Rehoboam to become king. There was all the fanfare as expected and the young man wisely chose to meet with his counselors. All the elders were there, and surprisingly enough Jeroboam was there as well. He had fled for his life to Egypt under the reign of Solomon, but now he felt secure enough to return to Jerusalem.

Rehoboam sat down on his throne and looked around the room at the elders. There wasn't a man there under the age of eighty. "Well," Rehoboam said, "what sort of advice do you gentlemen have for me?"

The first man gingerly stood up. "First off, Rehoboam, I just want to say it's a blessing to my old peepers to see you on your father's throne!"

"Your what?" Rehoboam said.

The old man continued talking. "I still remember when your grandpappy David was king. Yes sir those were the good old days."

"Yes, I'm sure they wer—" Rehoboam tried to interrupt but was completely unnoticed.

"Why, back then every man fought for his country, even the king, and every man loved his country," the old man said. This was followed by a chorus of *amens* and *that's right* from the other old men.

Another elder stood up, "Would you get on with it already, Ben Rama, before we all die of old age?"

The first elder snapped back, "Oh come off it, Ben Geyon. It's pretty clear that old age is *exactly* what we're going to die of!" to which everyone laughed except for Rehoboam who had his hand on his face.

"Anyways," Ben Rama said, "back to what I was talking about. What was I talking about?"

At this all the elders started talking and yelling and laughing.

"Oh lay off, will ya?" Ben Rama said, "I'm trying to help this ankle-biter out and keep him from making the same mistakes his daddy made!"

"Yes," Rehoboam said with a deep breath. "Please advise me. My father trusted you; I want to hear what you have to say."

"Listen up, whippersnapper: anyone can see that we can't just keep going on the way things have been. Your daddy was too hard on the people and you need to lighten the load."

"But my father was a great man," Rehoboam said.

"I oughta box your ears, boy! You been listenin' to those hippies too much! I'm telling ya a dying truth: those folks are just plain addicted to spending other people's money! You need to cut taxes or you're not going to have a kingdom!"

"That's right!" Ben Levy said.

"Amen!" Ben Tzaddik echoed.

"Hallelujah!" Ben Cohn hollered.

"Right on!" Ben Aaron cried.

"Right on?" Ben Rama said, looking back at Ben Aaron with a scowl.

"Sorry," Ben Aaron said, a little embarrassed.

Ben Rama cleared his throat and continued. "The point is clear son; you need to stop spending money like a blockhead or you'll regret it!"

There was a lull in the room, and then Rehoboam spoke. "Well, I thank you all for your colorful advice today. I'll be meeting with another group of men in a little while—men about my age, to discuss the state of the kingdom with them as well. You are all dismissed."

This was met with cacophony of protests from the elders.

"Don't listen to those beatniks!"

"They won't have anything good to say!"

"They'll just fool you with a bunch of malarkey!"

With all the commotion, Rehoboam didn't even notice the chilling voice that whispered in his ear. *Dismiss them, they can't help you. They're not relevant.*

Rehoboam raised his hand, "Yes, I'm sure. You are all dismissed."

Completely ignoring his command, the elders went on.

"Don't be bamboozled, boy! Lives are on the line here!"

"Those hippies just want to hornswoggle you!"

"Don't let them buffalo you, boy!"

"Don't be snookered!"

Rehoboam waved his hand and the guards came forward to usher the men out the door. As they did, one man somehow managed to stay to the side and as the others were going out the door, he stepped up to the king. This man was just as old as the others, but had been very quiet up to this point.

"Yes," Rehoboam said, letting his exasperation show a little.

"Son, we may seem a little old and senile to you, and our ways may seem a little backward, but your father was right when he said a gray head is a crown of glory. There's wisdom in what those men said. If you fall prey to smooth words and ignore scriptural advice just because you don't like the delivery, then you'll wind up like the fool your father wrote about."

The old men left, and Rehoboam made the same mistake his father had made. He ignored the counsel because he didn't like a message that didn't stroke his ego. The young men came in next and delivered their rousing speeches with their charts and illustrations. They were smooth and talked a lot about opportunity and vision and marketing new ideas and a bunch of other things the older men would have called hog-slop and hot-air.

And the old men were right. Rehoboam told the people he was raising taxes, they revolted, and that was that: the kingdom was split with the ten northern tribes siding with Jeroboam and the two southern tribes remaining with Rehoboam. There were now two kingdoms and two kings, just as Ahijah the prophet had foretold.

* * *

Months later in the northern kingdom, Jeroboam was listening to some counsel as well, only there were no other human beings in the room at the time.

"You're a fool if you think you'll be able to keep this throne," Satan whispered to Jeroboam.

"But Ahijah said it was mine, as long as I stayed faithful to the LORD," Jeroboam muttered.

"What would he know about leading a nation? He's a crotchety old man whose time has passed him by. You know what is going on in Jerusalem right now."

Jeroboam sighed. "Sacrifices."

"The heart follows the money, and if their money is going towards their religion, then that means their hearts are in Jerusalem. It's only a matter of time."

Satan was relentless in playing on the fears of the young man. *"They're going to go back to Rehoboam. They're going to go back to Jerusalem. What's that they say? If I forget thee, O Jerusalem, let my right hand forget her cunning? Your time is limited, Jeroboam, you had better act quickly."*

Day in and day out this would go on. The devil kept the king up at night with troubling thoughts and doubts. At any time Jeroboam could have called Ahijah in for counsel, but he didn't. Finally Jeroboam came to the conclusion that for the political separation to remain intact, a religious separation would be necessary.

And it was at that time that the religion of Nimrod, the religion of Baal, the golden bull, the sun god — the religion of Babylon, once again returned to Israel.

Chapter Thirty-Two

"For they that are such serve not our Lord Jesus Christ,
but their own belly; and by good words and fair
speeches deceive the hearts of the simple."
Romans 16:18

A year later near Bethel

The glory days of Israel were gone. In the southern kingdom Rehoboam held onto the worship of Jehovah, but in the ten northern tribes Jeroboam had resurrected within Israel the religion of Baal.

It was at this particular moment that a young man from the southern kingdom was riding his donkey north to confront Jeroboam. This young man was a prophet; he was a preacher who had served under the likes of great men like Ahijah. With the blush of youth still on his face he couldn't have been older than twenty-one or twenty-two. But his youth wasn't a detriment when it came to his delivery. If there was anything Ahijah had taught him, it was to deliver the message unafraid of their faces and to deliver every word of it.

He was in Ephraim's territory, entering into Bethel. Approaching the worship center, he could hear the sound of the music. "It's that cursed pagan music that Ahijah told me about. They have it thick up here," he muttered under his breath.

He wondered what the music was like in the early days of the temple. He was too young to have experienced that wonderful, fervent time in which the temple was dedicated under Solomon, and his soul longed to see revival in the land. The cheapness of idolatry and compromise in modern worship did nothing but infuriate him. He felt robbed and cheated, never knowing what others had taken for granted and tossed aside.

The young man stopped, tied his donkey to a tree, and stretched. He stroked the donkey's neck and said, "I'll be right back. This shouldn't take too long."

He didn't have to walk too far until he came upon the worship service of Jeroboam. There was everything that would be expected: the loud music, the naked dancing, the drunkenness, and right next to the altar was King Jeroboam in all his royal splendor getting ready to light up the incense.

The young man moved quickly taking long strides toward the altar, and everyone fanned away from him. He hadn't said anything yet, but he had a look about him that screamed that he was a prophet of Jehovah.

He held up his right hand in the prophetic salute and cried aloud, "O altar, altar, thus saith the LORD: Behold, a child shall be born unto the house of David, Josiah by name; and upon thee shall he offer the priests of the high places that burn incense upon thee, and men's bones shall be burnt upon thee!"

"What?!?" Jeroboam said.

"I said a child of the house of David is going to burn the bones of your priests on this altar!"

"That's ridiculous!" Jeroboam said and all those gathered around started laughing.

Unphased, the young man raised his hand again. "This is the sign which the LORD hath spoken; Behold, the altar shall be rent, and the ashes that are upon it shall be poured out."

Jeroboam was irate. "I've had enough of this! We don't go around saying bad things about your religion down there in Jerusalem! You have your religion and we have ours!"

He pointed at the young man and looked over to soldiers that were nearby, "Grab that kid and bring him over here."

And then it happened. Jeroboam gasped, and his eyes grew wide, and he fell to his knees. Everyone was stunned; something strange was happening to the king's arm. It was stiff, frozen in place, as if rigormortis had set in even though he was very much alive. The king screamed as the muscles in his arm seized and hardened.

His job complete, the young man turned and started to walk away. Just then a loud cracking noise was heard and the altar behind Jeroboam split in half and all the ashes flew up into the air. Jeroboam, wincing in pain on his knees and covered in ashes, held his arm out to the prophet.

"Wait!" he cried out. "Don't leave me like this! Pray for me! Pray that the LORD would heal me!"

The young man stopped and turned around. He looked at the crowd and then bowed his head. Everyone else awkwardly bowed their heads as well. "LORD, this man would like to be healed. He doesn't deserve it, but then again none of us deserve your mercy or grace. LORD, for your glory, and if you are willing, would you heal him? Amen."

Jeroboam gasped again. "I'm healed! He did it! The LORD healed me! Praise the LORD everyone, praise the LORD!"

The eyes of the people grew wide with astonishment and they all uneasily said their own *amens*.

The prophet turned again to walk away but Jeroboam called out to him. "Wait! Wait, young man, wait. I want to thank you. Thanks for setting me straight on that whole thing. I've never been a real religious man, but Ahijah, well, he put me in this spot, and it looks like I really messed things up."

The prophet just looked at him.

Jeroboam went on. "I guess what I'm trying to say is that I'm sorry, and I'm gonna clean up my act. It's Jehovah or bust from hereon out."

"I see," the prophet said.

"Well, um," Jeroboam stammered, "how about you come in for a bite to eat? We've got some good food, some good bread to eat, and some water. It's a long journey back. Come take a break. I'd like to give you a reward as well."

"No sir, no way, no how," the prophet said. "Thanks, but the LORD told me not to stop to eat bread or drink water on this journey. I'm not about to walk in the counsel of the ungodly, or stand in the way of sinners, or sit in the seat of the scornful. You could promise me half your house and it wouldn't be enough to get me to go back on the word of the LORD."

"I hear you loud and clear!" Jeroboam said with a smile and patted the prophet on the back.

Uncomfortable at the physical touch the prophet shrugged Jeroboam's hand off his shoulder. "Very well then. Goodbye, Jeroboam, and may you stay true to Jehovah from hereon out. Blessed is the nation whose God is the LORD."

And with that, he saddled his donkey and began the trip back to Jerusalem.

* * *

"Father! You wouldn't believe what happened!" the boys said as they crashed through the front door, completely destroying the peaceful silence that the old man had been enjoying by himself.

He sighed, set his drink down, cocked a half-smile, and looked up at them. "Try me."

They all started at once, causing him to close his eyes and hold up his hand. A moment passed, then the oldest began to speak. "There was a prophet, a young prophet, and he rebuked the king. The king's hand froze up and then the prophet healed him!"

"You mean God healed him," the old man replied, taking a sip from his drink.

"Yes, God healed him. And then the king said he was sorry about the golden calf and that he wouldn't do it again!"

"Interesting. Where was the prophet from?"

"I don't know, somewhere in the southern kingdom though. He must have traveled a long way! He's headed by our house!"

The old man's disposition brightened at this news. "That's wonderful! Get my donkey ready! I want to go and meet this young man! What a blessing!"

"Yes sir!" the boys said in excitement and ran back out the door. Except for one, that lingered a moment longer.

"Father," he said.

"Yes son?"

"Why did God have that prophet travel so far to speak to the king, when he could have just asked you?"

The father took a long drink from his cup, set it down, and looked out through the door the boys had left open. "That's a good question, son. That's a good question."

* * *

The young prophet sat resting under a mighty oak tree when the old man appeared.

"Why hello there, young fella! Are you the prophet that told off Jeroboam?" he said excitedly.

"I suppose you could put it that way," the young man replied.

"I have to say, young man, when my children told me the story of what happened, it thrilled my soul!"

"Oh?" the young man said, standing up.

"Yes sir!" the older man said with a twinkle in his eyes. "How about you come over to my place for a bite to eat and we can swap stories a little?"

"I can't; I'm sorry. The LORD instructed me to not stop to eat or drink on my way home, or to take the same way home that I took here the first time."

The older man paused for awhile, and then he smiled. "You don't have to worry about that, son. I'm a prophet just as you are, and an angel told me that the LORD actually wants you to come and visit with me. The LORD told me that he wants you to come over to my place, take a break, eat some bread and have a drink of water. The LORD just didn't want you to be tempted by Jeroboam to eat with him."

The young man thought for a moment. "All right, well, I suppose if you're a prophet and the LORD told you that, I'd be happy to come and visit with you."

"Great!" the older man said as he got back on his donkey to lead the way.

"So you're a prophet you said," spoke the young man as he followed behind.

"I sure am! There were many times when I had to deliver a message just like you did at the altar."

"I see. Ahijah never mentioned you."

"Well, that's probably because we didn't run in the same circles, you know. Ahijah is a good man, but he and I don't see eye-to-eye on a few things. I'm sure you understand," the older man said as he ducked under a branch.

"Sure, I suppose so."

"Son, we all have our own road in life to follow, and mine took me a different path than Ahijah. He's a, well, a bit too strict for me; a bit too literal, if you know what I mean."

"I'm not sure I do."

"Well, he's a literalist, and tends to focus more on the details of things. And that's fine! I'm just a little more open-minded to the grand scheme of things and the end of a matter not just the beginning. I try to take the long look and focus on the big picture. As Solomon said, 'Where there is no vision, the people perish.'"

"I see," the young man said.

The older man laughed. "I'm not trying to bad-mouth old Ahijah! He's a good man and we need more like him!"

"That's the truth!" the young man said.

It didn't take long to arrive at the old man's house. The young prophet was pleased to take a rest and rubbed his hands and smiled as the hot bread was placed on the table.

"Smells just like home!" he said.

"Good! I'm hungry too!" the old man said with a smile.

They prayed and then dove right into their meal, all the while telling stories back and forth about serving the LORD. Then something started to happen. The old man stopped talking and the conversation became one-sided. After awhile the young man stopped talking as well, and then there was silence.

The old man stood to his feet, right there in the middle of the meal, and raised his hand to speak the word of the LORD. "Thus saith the LORD, Forasmuch as thou hast disobeyed the mouth of the LORD, and hast not kept the commandment which the LORD thy God commanded thee, but camest back, and hast eaten bread and drunk water in the place, of the which the LORD did say to thee, Eat no bread, and drink no water; thy carcase shall not come unto the sepulchre of thy fathers."

The young man choked down his food. "What?!?!"

"You're going to die for disobeying the word of the LORD, young man. You're not even going to make it home," the old man said.

"But you said it was okay! I trusted you!"

"I lied to you, son."

The young man of God was confused and irate. "Why? Why would you do that? My blood is on your hands, you old fool!"

"I, I, I don't know," the old man stammered. "I think I just didn't think it was that important. I just didn't think it really made any difference whether or not you ate on the way."

"The difference is that God told me not to; that's the difference! I trusted you!" he said with a broken and frustrated heart. "You're an old preacher; if I can't trust an old preacher in this sad and wicked world, then who can I trust?"

"I'm sorry son; I'm sorry."

"You're sorry, but I'm the one who's going to die. I have to deal with the consequences of my decision because I'm the one who made it."

The older man sat staring at his food. "Ahijah taught you well. I don't have enough respect for the word of the LORD, but he always did."

The young man finished his bread and water and stood up. "Goodbye," he said and walked out the door, ready to take his penalty like a man.

After about thirty minutes the old man got on his donkey and followed the path that he knew the young man took. He found him dead on the road, with the lion standing guard by his body, and the donkey still alive.

"Alas, my brother!" he said with a broken heart, picking up the body and placing it on his donkey to take home.

And it came to pass, after he had buried him, that he spake to his sons, saying, "When I am dead, then bury me in the sepulchre wherein the man of God is buried; lay my bones beside his bones."

Chapter Thirty-Three

**"For *his* letters, say they, *are* weighty and powerful; but
his bodily presence *is* weak, and *his* speech
contemptible."
II Corinthians 10:10**

951 B.C. Shiloh

The years had passed and Ahijah, the fiery preacher from the country, had grown old. He stooped when he walked. He used a walking stick, and his voice trembled when he spoke. He would still go into the city to minister, but he didn't preach often anymore because he simply didn't have the strength to do it. Eventually he came to the point where he rarely left his home because of his failing eyesight. Nearing the twilight of his life now, people came to him to seek wisdom and the word of the LORD.

But then there was Jeroboam. Jeroboam had destroyed the religion of the Northern Kingdom, and his pagan worship had already seeped into Judah as well. God had stayed his hand of judgment long enough, but now the gavel had fallen and the first victim was Jeroboam's son, Abijah. The young boy had become deathly ill. Under the instructions of her husband, Jeroboam's wife was now approaching the old prophet to ask him what to do; only she was disguised as a simple commoner.

"Come on in," Ahijah said as he heard her feet pausing at the door.

The door creaked as she walked in, and looking around, she saw the old prophet sitting on a chair with his back to her.

"You don't need to be disguised. I know who you are," he said softly.

"You do?" she said. "Well, of course you do. Ahijah, my son is sick, and Jeroboam sent me to—"

Ahijah held up his hand. "I know why you're here. You're here because Jeroboam is too cowardly to talk to the old man who showed him the right way twenty-four years ago."

The woman swallowed hard and offered no argument.

"Listen lady, I have heavy tidings for you. I'm not going to sugar-coat it for you or water it down. Jeroboam isn't here to hear it, so you're just going to have to pass it on to him."

She looked, and her gut tightened with a mixture of horror and astonishment as she saw the old man's trembling right hand lift into the air with his index finger pointing up in the sign of the prophet. She knew what followed was a message from the LORD.

"Thus saith the LORD," he said, his voice much stronger now. "Forasmuch as I exalted thee from among the people, and made thee prince over my people Israel, and rent the kingdom away from the house of David, and gave it thee: and yet thou hast not been as my servant David.

"But thou, Jeroboam, hast done evil above all those that were before thee. Thou hast cast me behind thy back and made other gods and molten images and provoked me to anger."

Ahijah knew the woman was crying by now, but nothing was going to stop him from delivering the message that God told him to deliver, exactly how God told him to deliver it, regardless of the audience.

"Therefore, because thou hast done evil above all those before thee, I will cut off from Jeroboam's house all those that piss against the wall. Every male will be taken away as a man takes away dung from his land."

She was repulsed; she was shocked, and she was sobbing. She was royal blood, the wife of a king, and no one had ever spoken to her this way.

Ahijah went on. "Those of Jeroboam's line that die in the city shall the dogs eat, and in the field shall the birds of the air eat: for the LORD hath spoken it.

"Arise and go to thy house. When thy feet shall enter the city, the child shall die. All Israel shall mourn for him and bury him, because in him was found some good thing toward the LORD God of Israel. The LORD shall raise him up a king in Israel that shall wipe out the line of Jeroboam; and the LORD shall smite Israel as a reed shaken in the water, and he shall scatter them."

The woman left in a rage, slamming the door behind her and leaving the prophet alone, once again, in his house.

He sighed. He looked out the window. He closed his eyes and rubbed his temples. Then he sighed again.

"What is it, Ahijah?" the LORD said.

"LORD, you know the thoughts and intents of my heart better than I do," he said.

"I'd just like to hear you tell me what you think it is."

"I think I'm just tired, LORD."

"At your age you're always tired, Ahijah," the LORD said.

Ahijah smiled. "I supposed I'm a little discouraged too, LORD."

"Go on. Tell me about it."

"Well, LORD, I'm just tired of giving people rotten messages. I mean, why did I have to tell her that? Why'd you want me to be so crude about it?"

"Well, in this case I did that so that preachers in the Laodicean age could be encouraged to preach a little harder when people will give them a hard time for taking a stand on things. They can always take comfort in the fact that I didn't ask them to say what I just asked you to say."

"What?"

"Never mind, go on."

"Well, LORD, I'm just tired of things going south on me. Solomon messed up. Rehoboam messed up. Jeroboam messed up. Things just keep getting worse and worse."

"Yes," the LORD said.

"And I'm tired of people not listening to what I keep telling them! Don't people know that things go better for them when they just listen to the preacher? They look at me and nod like a cow looking at a new fence, and then they go out and do the complete opposite!"

"Well, Ahijah, you'd feel a lot better if you'd quit trying to do my job and just stuck to your own."

This snapped Ahijah out of his momentary stupor. "What?"

"It's not anything you don't already know, preacher. It's not anything you haven't taught your students before. Your job ends after you deliver the message."

"But LORD, sometimes—"

"I know, there are exceptions to that from time to time. But you preachers tend to forget that I called you to preach, not to worry. I didn't call you to be a politician or a psychologist; I called you to be a preacher."

"Yes LORD. But you'll have to forgive me for this," Ahijah sighed, "I sure would have liked to have been a prophet under David—"

"You mean when he was running for his life from Saul? During the dark days of his kingdom following his adultery? Perhaps when he had to leave the throne or when his children were killing each other?"

"Hmmmm," Ahijah said.

"Hmmmm is right," the LORD said. "The good old days are never as good as anyone ever thinks they are."

"Yeah, I suppose so."

"It's a lot better if you just do your job and let me take care of the rest, right?"

"Yes, LORD."

"You do know I'm going to keep my promises, right? You do know you have a home on the other side, and the day will come when this land will flow with my righteousness, and my king will rule, right?"

"Yes, LORD."

"Then think on those things."

Chapter Thirty-Four

"And he answered him, I *am:* go, tell thy lord, Behold,
Elijah *is here.*"
I Kings 18:8

910 B.C. Jezreel

Time wore on and Ahijah passed away and so did Jeroboam. Israel, the northern kingdom, as a whole remained in a state of rotten apostasy. The idolatry of Jeroboam remained strong, so strong, in fact, that from time to time Israel actually went to war with Judah over the issue of religion.

Down south in Judah, things were much better. Judah had a good king in Asa, and subsequently another good king in his son Jehoshaphat. Jehoshaphat loved the LORD, had removed many of the altars in the high places, and had gone to war with some of the surrounding heathen nations. In time God had given Judah peace, but in his quest for peace Jehoshaphat eventually allowed his son to marry the daughter of the king of Israel.

That king, the king of Israel, was a king that had managed to do more to provoke the anger of Jehovah than even Jeroboam had done. The sun god Baalite religion had not only flourished under the reign of Ahab, it had become the state religion. The true worshipers of Jehovah hid for their lives from the tyranny of Ahab and his Phoenician wife, Jezebel.

The state-sanctioned worship of Baal was a horrible thing. Mothers were forced to sacrifice their own children to please this wrathful god that others might bear more children. There were elaborate temples and alters established for the prostitution of their daughters, and the people performed vile worship ceremonies of bestiality and fornication.

It was another day in the midst of this wanton debauchery that found Ahab and Jezebel in the throne room of Israel enjoying a nice meal together. They laid on their sides eating all manner of food during that afternoon meal, some of which was forbidden under the Hebrew law. They enjoyed the music and the fanning of palm leaves. Everything was as it should be, up until a rather rude and unexpected event should occur.

The doors flew open with an obnoxious crash, and a strange looking man suddenly entered the room. He was a very thin and wiry man, not an ounce of fat on him, with dark olive-colored skin. He wore a leather girdle that came right above his knees, carried a mean-looking rod, and had a dark brown beard. He flashed a crooked and amused grin on his face as he strolled right up to the king.

"Why hello, Your Majesty!" the man said with a bow.

"Who are you?" Ahab said, unamused with the peculiar stranger.

"I'm the reason you haven't had rain for the last six months," he said, grunting as he stretched to touch his toes.

Ahab popped a grape into his mouth. "That's interesting. Why are you doing calisthenics in my throne room?"

The gangly man chuckled. "Because you're not going to like what I have to say next and as Ahijah used to put it *'somma da time a good prophet needs ta absquatulate after delivering a message.'*

"I think we call that an exit strategy," Ahab said as he shoved a piece of bacon in his mouth. "Want some bacon?"

"No sir, wrong dispensation," he said, swinging his arms in a circle and hopping on his toes.

"Well, let's have it then," Ahab said.

The man stopped and raised his hand in the prophetic salute, his voice now loud enough to be heard throughout the entire palace. "King Ahab, my name is Elijah the Tishbite! As the LORD God of Israel liveth, before whom I stand, there shall not be dew nor rain these years, but according to my word."

Ahab coughed on his bacon and motioned with his off hand. "Well then, we had better not let you leave!"

Elijah smiled. "I thought you might say that, pleased to make your acquaintance and all, but I think I'll be absquatulating now."

Four guards approached Elijah in a pincer movement from the rear. Their swords were sheathed as they intended to capture the prophet, not kill him. With amazing quickness Elijah high-stepped to the right and avoided the first man as he dove to grab him. Then Elijah rammed his shoulder into the chest of the second man and spun off of him, heading for the doors at the back of the room. The next man grasped at Elijah to no avail. The prophet would simply not stop moving his feet; twisting and turning, he wiggled away again. The last man stood at the door, blocking the wiry man's exit. Quite unexpectedly, Elijah hit the man across the side of the head with his rod, and ran out the door.

Ahab sighed, and reached for another piece of bacon.

Elijah ran and ran and ran. Other than preaching, the one thing that Elijah was really good at was running.

The LORD spoke to Elijah in a still small voice. *Run east, Elijah, and hide by the brook Cherith, which is by Jordan. The ravens will feed you there.*

"Yes, LORD! I'll get right over there!" Elijah said as he jumped over a log and ducked under a tree. The palace guards were hot on his trail but they didn't really have much of a chance to catch him. The man ran like a gazelle. He ran, and he ran, and he ran, and he ran, and rarely did he ever stop to take a breath. No one really knows how long it took Elijah to get to the stream, but everyone knows he arrived there faster than anyone else could.

And when Elijah finally did reach the stream he tossed his rod under a tree and sat down on his haunches to drink from the stream. Smiling, he took a deep breath and gazed in the water. "Well LORD, what do you want me to do now?"

Eat.

"Well, if you really want me to, that's fine; but I'd just as soon go deliver another message! Want me to run back to the palace again, or maybe go tell off some of the Baalite priests for you, LORD?"

Now Elijah, I love your zeal, but when I say to take a rest and eat, you need to obey me.

"Oh, of course, LORD."

Elijah looked around and saw a few trees, a lot of dirt and sand, and water. "Um, LORD, what am I supposed to eat?"

I'm working on that. One moment please.

"Yes, LORD," Elijah said as he sat down under the tree by his rod.

Life up your head, Elijah, for your lunch draweth nigh.

Elijah looked up and saw one of the strangest things he'd ever seen. Up in the sky, he saw several rows of ravens, and they were carrying a dinner plate supported by dozens of strings. They flew right up to Elijah and dropped the plate on the ground. Elijah looked at the plate and saw cooked chicken and quail, and some hot soft bread.

"Thank you, LORD."

You're welcome, Elijah. Did you see the seal on the plate?

Elijah looked under the bread and smiled when he saw the seal of the king of Israel.

"Is this Ahab's dinner?"

That WAS Ahab's dinner, the LORD said.

Elijah leaned back and laughed 'till his stomach hurt. "LORD, serving you is a lot more fun than anything else a guy could do!"

I'm glad you're enjoying yourself. Now eat up, go to sleep, and I'll have breakfast in the morning for you.

"But no bacon, right?" Elijah said with a smile.

That's right, no special dispensation for you.

Chapter Thirty-Five

"But *let it be* the hidden man of the heart, in that which is not corruptible, *even the ornament* of a meek and quiet spirit, which is in the sight of God of great price."
I Peter 3:4

A couple months later by the Brook Cherith

Elijah enjoyed his time by the river over the next couple months. Having more energy than he knew what to do with, he was constantly coming up with physical activities. He'd climb trees and do sit-ups off the branches. He invented the jump-rope. He built a house, tore it down, and then built a better house. He took up pole-vaulting. Why? Well, the way Elijah figured, he always carried around a rod because it was the prophetly thing to do, and pole-vaulting might actually come in handy one day.

And in all his physically-straining and absolutely-exhausting activities from which he was never really tired, Elijah started to notice one thing. The water was running out in the brook.

"LORD," Elijah said as he was casually doing pull-ups, "the water is running out."

Well, that's what happens when it doesn't rain.

"I suppose so," Elijah said while doing a back-flip from off the branch and sticking the landing. "I'm guessing it hasn't been three years yet, and I'm not supposed to ask you to let it rain now, am I?"

No, you're not supposed to ask me to let it rain, and no it hasn't been a total of three and a half years since I asked you to ask me to stop the rain.

"Ok, well, do you need me to go do anything or should I just keep myself busy?"

Head on over to Zarephath, I want you to live with a widow woman. She'll take care of you now.

Running to Zarephath, Elijah was undecided if learning pole-vaulting was really worth all the work he had put into it. After all, he reasoned, he could have taught himself various methods of self-defense that involved a rod. It was about that time that he caught his second wind and was able to go from a casual sprint to a really fast sprint. He shrugged off his internal debate with the conclusion that the next time God would have him live alone by a brook he'd focus on his Bo Staff skills.

Nearing the gate of the city he came upon the widow woman.

"Hi there, are you the widow woman?" he called from a distance as soon as he saw her.

"Well," she said as he drew near. "I'm *a* widow woman. There are others, you know."

"I suppose so, but you'll do," Elijah said. "Can you please go get me something to drink?"

Coming from a smelly, sweaty, and strange looking man dressed in camel clothes, it was a rather odd and forward question she thought. Actually, it was a pretty forward question coming from anyone she further considered. But this widow woman was a cut above your average person. She remembered a story from the scriptures about a woman named Rebekah who gave water to a stranger and in the end wound up marrying a handsome rich guy because of it.

"Sure, I'll go get it for you," she said as she ran off.

"Thanks," he called to her as she left. "Can you bring me some bread too while you're at it?"

She stopped. As she turned around to speak with him, all the prior zeal and excitement immediately drained from her. It was in that moment that reality hit her: she was starving, and so was her son.

She was nervous in her reply, and she couldn't help but tremble. "I don't know who you are, and I'd be happy to help you, but my son and I are starving. I don't have any bread. I can make some bread, but what little meal and oil I have left I was going to use for me and my son's last meal. We're going to eat it, and then we're going to die."

"Don't be afraid," Elijah said, waving his hand dismissively. "Go ahead and do whatever you were planning on doing, but feed me first then make some food for you and your son. God said you weren't going to run out of meal or oil until it starts to rain again."

Are you completely out of your mind? I'm starving to death but I'm supposed to just take your word for it and feed you first? You're a Jew and I'm a Gentile! You're dressed like a lunatic and I don't even know your name!

That's not what she said, of course; it's just merely some of what passed through her mind during the handful of heartbeats that followed his request.

She smiled and said, "I'll get to work on that meal for you right now."

And it was that enormous amount of faith that the woman showed that day that saved her life and the life of her son. She took care of Elijah the next couple of years, and God took care of her. Before the three and a half year mark had come up, another miracle was done in that the widow's boy died and was raised to life again. Elijah cried unto the LORD and stretched himself upon the child three times, and his soul returned unto him again.

Such was the life of Elijah, and he enjoyed his brief time of peace and rest with the widow and her son.

Chapter Thirty-Six

"For I have not shunned to declare unto you all the counsel of God."
Acts 20:27

906 B.C. On the road to Jezreel

Now all the time that Elijah was hiding from the king, there was another fellow that wasn't. Not only was this other fellow not hiding from King Ahab, but he was actually a man of high position and rank within the house of Ahab. If one didn't know any better, and most people didn't know any better, one would never know that this man was a worshipper of Jehovah and not of Baal.

This man's name was Obadiah, not to be confused with another Obadiah that would arrive on the scene hundreds of years later preaching hellfire and judgment—that was the last thing you'd ever find this Obadiah doing.

Don't get the wrong idea though, Obadiah loved the LORD. In fact, he even feared the LORD. You see, while other prophets were running and hiding because they took a public stand for God, in many cases it was Obadiah that was giving the prophets refuge and food. He was a good man, and God used him.

And it was right about this time that on a road by himself Obadiah ran into the complete opposite of himself: Elijah. When Obadiah rounded the corner and saw the crooked grin of Elijah there to greet him, it simply took his breath away. Immediately he fell on his face.

"Are you Elijah?" Obadiah said from the ground, peeking up.

"You know who I am. Get up here and talk to me like a man!" Elijah snorted.

"Well Elijah," Obadiah said, "you are the type to shoot first and ask questions later, so I thought the prudent thing to do was—"

"Bah! Prudence is overrated," Elijah snorted, again.

"Exactly my point," Obadiah said, dusting himself off.

"All right, all right," Elijah said, "I need you to go and tell your lord that Elijah is coming to see him."

"Certainly, but you know of course that Jehovah is my real LORD, right?"

"Could have fooled me, little buddy," Elijah said.

"What?" Obadiah said indignantly, "Do you think you're the only prophet out here? While you're taking it easy eating with the Gentiles, I've been risking my life every day and night to feed a hundred prophets in a cave."

Elijah kicked his head back and laughed. "You've got some spirit to you, and a lot of gall! You must really be suffering for Jehovah living the life of luxury in that palace!"

Obadiah gasped. "It grieves my righteous soul to be in there, but that's where God wants me!"

"Oh yeah man, you're real righteous!" Elijah said, and then glanced at Obadiah's midsection. "In fact, if you keep packing on the pounds in that place you'll be twice the prophet I am!"

Obadiah sucked in his belly. "I'm not a prophet; I'm a humble servant of the LORD. Not everyone is called to dress like a maniac and holler at everything that moves, you know."

"You're a compromiser," Elijah said. "Know ye not that friendship with the world is enmity with God? How can two walk together except they be agreed? Figure out who you really love and who you really fear and then come talk to me."

"Elijah, were the Hebrew midwives backslidden when they hid the baby boys? The word says that a prudent man foreseeth the evil, and hideth himself; but the simple pass on, and are punished. It says to give subtilty to the simple, to the young man knowledge and discretion. It also says—"

"It also says the serpent was more subtil than any beast of the field," Elijah interrupted, "and that Amnon's friend Jonadab was a very subtil man. And it also says that the harlot was subtil of heart. I prefer a man that just puts it out there in the open and lets God sort things out."

"Elijah, I'm doing the best I can not to be a friend to the world, and I certainly don't want to be at enmity with God. I'm in the midst of wolves. I'm just trying to be harmless as a dove, and wise as a serpent."

Elijah scratched his beard and thought. "That harmless dove and wise serpent bit—is that scripture?"

"Not that I know of," Obadiah said.

"Well, it oughta be; it's pretty good," Elijah said with a smile.

Obadiah smiled back. "That friendship with the world is enmity with God part is pretty good too, brother."

Obadiah started to turn away and then paused. "Elijah?"

"Yes?" Elijah said turning back.

"You're not going to leave me high and dry on this, are you?"

"What do you mean?"

"Well," Obadiah said, looking at the ground, "if Ahab comes out here to meet you and you're not here— I'm as good as dead. You understand?"

Elijah sighed. "Obadiah, maybe I need to learn a little couth and grace and all that stuff, but you need to get some guts. Trust God a little, son. As the LORD of Hosts liveth, before whom I stand, I will surely show myself unto him this day."

"That's good enough for me," Obadiah said. He turned, this time to go and pass the message onto Ahab.

Time was up.

Chapter Thirty-Seven

"And it came to pass at noon, that Elijah mocked them,
and said, Cry aloud: for he *is* a god; either he is talking,
or he is pursuing, or he is in a journey, *or* peradventure
he sleepeth, and must be awaked."
I Kings 18:27

906 B.C. Jezreel

Ahab got off his horse, red-faced and shaking his finger at Elijah. "It's you! You've been troubling Israel! My people are starving and dying of thirst because of you!"

"You're the one who's troubling Israel," Elijah said as he took a couple steps toward the king. "Your people are fornicating in the fields and sacrificing their children to Baal trying to get it to rain, because that's what your wife taught them to do! You're a king of Israel. What business did you have marrying that Phoenician whore?

"You're the one who's troubled Israel—you and your father's house! You're a strong man. You could have been a strong leader if you'd chosen the LORD over politics, you fool! You've forsaken the commandments of the LORD and you've followed Baal."

Ahab started to say something, but Elijah, who was on a roll, interrupted him before he could. "We're going to settle this today, Your Majesty! You want some rain? We'll get some rain one way or another. Get your wife's black-robbed Baalite buffoon prophets to Mount Carmel, and meet me there. Get everyone there! Get all of Israel there!"

* * *

The time had come, and all of Israel was gathered at Mount Carmel to see the great contest between Elijah and the prophets of Baal.

"It's your funeral when this is all over," Ahab said to Elijah, "so go ahead and say whatever you have to say."

It was about this time that one might expect a lengthy prophety-type message that would gear up to a grand crescendo of conviction in which droves of people would make a decision for Jehovah. But this was Elijah, and he just decided to skip to the end and went straight to the invitation.

"All right listen up you bunch of stiffnecked and rebellious Jews!" Elijah said. "How long are you going to halt between two opinions? If the LORD be God, then follow him! If Baal is God, then follow him.

"Every eye closed and every head bowed."

About half the people just looked around, wide-eyed and awkward. The other half bowed their heads and peeked through their fingers to see what was going on.

"All right, anyone here want to get right?" Elijah said.

Nothing happened.

"Anyone need prayer for anything?"

There was a cough, and more people bowed their heads to avoid the chance of eye contact with the preacher.

"Does anyone want to rededicate their lives to the LORD?" Elijah said, exasperated.

Elijah sighed. *Preach an amazing message and no one comes forward—story of my life.* "All right, All right everyone look up here!"

Everyone breathed a sigh of relief and looked up at the preacher.

"I'm the only prophet of the LORD here. There are four hundred and fifty of Baal's prophets here. They're going to get a bull, and I'm going to get a bull, and we're

going to sacrifice them. They're going to call out for Baal;
I'm going to pray to Jehovah. Whoever answers with fire
is God."

"Amen!" the people said.

"Amen!" Elijah said back with a smile. "Now we're
getting somewhere! Being the gentleman that you all
know me to be, I'm going to give the Baalite boys the first
go."

After dressing the bull and preparing the altar, the
prophets started some rather odd rituals. First they got
in little huddles and confessed their sins to each other
and forgave each other. Then they pulled out necklaces
with beads on them and prayed to the beads. Then they
broke out crackers, held them up to the sun, prayed to
them, and then fed them to each other.

Elijah cleared his throat in a not-so-subtle manner.
"Any day now, fellas."

"You're interrupting our sacred sanctimoniousness!"

"Your what?"

"Never mind. Please allow us to perform our rituals
without interruption."

"I'll do my best, but I'd rather not be here all day,"
Elijah said.

Then there were the prayers, and my oh my were
they repetitious.

"OH Baal, hear us."

"Hear US Baal, hear us."

"HEAR us, Baal."

"Baal, hear US."

"Hear US here, Baal."

"Here US hear, Baal."

"If there's anything I can't stand its bad grammar," Elijah muttered to some nameless person next to him.

This went on and on and on, and the fire didn't fall. The prophets became desperate. One of them produced a jar with shards of glass, and he poured it on the ground. The other prophets crawled on their knees and cried out to Baal while the first prophet whipped them. It was pathetic; it was frantic; it was sad, but to Elijah it was funny.

"Speak louder, boys! He can't hear you!" Elijah said.

So they screamed louder. "Hear us, Baal! Hear us!"

Elijah leaned back and laughed. "Maybe he's up there with the Queen of Heaven and can't hear you over her nagging! Speak up!"

The prophets glared at Elijah, and screaming all the more they jumped up on the altar. They pulled out knives and began cutting themselves.

"Oh boy!" Elijah laughed. "Baal better do something fast before you fools all bleed to death! Maybe he's on a long trip, or maybe he's taking a nap and you need to wake him up!"

It went on and on, the constant screaming and cutting and Elijah's mocking. Finally, the priests of Baal stopped. They were finished; they were exhausted, and nothing had happened.

Finally, the Baalite prophets collapsed in a heap around their altar, and all eyes turned to Elijah.

Elijah clapped his hands and smiled. "All right! My turn!" He then walked over to the side where there was an old altar that had been broken down.

"God commanded you to worship and sacrifice in Jerusalem; however your forefathers broke that command before and after the kingdom split. In the wars that followed between your kingdom and Judah many were prevented from worshipping and sacrificing in Jerusalem. God, in his mercy, winked at this transgression. Today, he allows another altar to be built to him. He is the one true God; he is merciful and gracious to his people."

Elijah pushed over the rocks and found twelve new stones. As he spoke to the people he tirelessly and quickly built a trench around the altar, put the wood on the altar, and cut up the bullock for sacrifice. "Today this altar is repaired and dedicated to the LORD God Jehovah. Today may you repair the altars of your hearts to the LORD, and God in his mercy will accept you. He will forgive your transgressions."

The people were moved by the message, and it was a great time to have an invitation, but instead Elijah decided to have water dumped on the altar.

"Okay, somebody fill up four barrels of water and dump it all over the sacrifice and the wood."

"This has to be the strangest prophet ever," one of the four men said as he and the others manned the cart to bring the water to the altar. As they dumped the water on the sacrifice, Elijah preached some more.

"That's the washing of water by the word, Israel! You need some repentance! Dump more water on there!"

So they dumped water on the altar a second time.

"Do it a third time!" Elijah said.

They dumped water on it a third time and it soaked the bullock, the wood, and ran off the altar and filled the trench with water.

Elijah backed a safe distance from the altar, fell to his knees, closed his eyes, and raised his hands to the heavens. "LORD God of Abraham, Isaac, and of Israel, let it be known this day that thou art God in Israel; and that I am thy servant, and that I have done all these things at thy word.

Hear me, O LORD. Hear me, that this people may know that thou art the LORD God, and that thou hast turned their heart back again."

There was no cutting of flesh, no dancing around, no lathering up of emotions, and no vain repetitions. It was a short, concise, and powerful prayer by a man who'd been living in the center of God's will for years.

The sky darkened, the clouds spread apart, and a blast of fire steamed down from heaven and struck the sacrifice squarely in the center of the altar. The fire spread and consumed the sacrifice, the wood, the stones, the dust, and even licked up the water. The sudden heat pushed everyone back and caused them to cover their eyes and faces. Elijah stood up and turned to the people; but before he could speak, they all fell to their faces and cried out together:

"The LORD! He is the God! The LORD! He is the God!"

Ahab was in stunned silence, and he was reeling in confusion and frustration from the whole scene. His wife's prophets— his prophets, had failed. They were exhausted and at this moment trying to metaphorically sneak out the back door. Elijah, the man he had denounced for the last three years as public enemy number one, had just won the day. The people had just repented and proclaimed Jehovah to be the God, and Elijah was in charge.

Elijah gave the order, "Take the prophets of Baal, and don't let them escape!" The people obeyed and brought them to the brook Kishon, and there was a great slaughter. All four hundred fifty of the Baalite priests were slain, and their bodies tossed to the side for the birds of the sky to eat.

"Time to eat, Ahab," Elijah said, noting the confusion and fatigue in his eyes. "Go eat and drink. It's been a long day. The rain is coming. There is the sound of abundance of rain; prepare for the latter rain."

Then Ahab staggered to his chariot and his servants brought him food. As Ahab started to eat, Elijah turned to climb up Mount Carmel again. He was tired, and other than a servant that was assigned to help him, he was alone. "Go and look towards the sea," Elijah said to the servant as he got to his knees and put his face to the ground.

The man returned. "There's nothing unusual to see," he said.

"Do it again. Look toward the sea and tell me what you observe," Elijah said.

This was repeated seven times until the man returned. "I see a small cloud; it looks like a man's hand. It's coming from the sea."

Elijah stood up and dusted himself off. "Go and tell Ahab to leave now, so that the rain doesn't hinder him."

Upon hearing the order, Ahab's chariot lurched forward and began the trip to Jezreel. As he rode off, the clouds turned dark and the winds began to blow, and then the rain started to fall. All through the land of Israel the people laughed and wept as the healing water fell from the sky. The children rolled around in the puddles as their mothers and fathers danced in the streets. The times of refreshing had come.

And up on Mount Carmel, Elijah was alone. He had dismissed the servant, and he stood there by himself.

"Well, LORD, what do you want me to do now?"

Elijah couldn't see God, and he couldn't touch God, but right now he could feel God. He felt God smile.

Elijah, right now I want you to do what you love to do, and what you're especially good at.

"What's that, LORD?"

Run.

Chapter Thirty-Eight

"Elias was a man subject to like passions as we are, and he prayed earnestly that it might not rain: and it rained not on the earth by the space of three years and six months."
James 5:17

906 B.C. Mount Carmel

And run he did. The same Holy Spirit that came upon Samson and gave him the strength to kill a thousand Philistines came upon Elijah at that moment. After an exhausting day both physically and spiritually, Elijah could feel his entire body surge with energy. His mind was clear, his body felt loose and warm, and his spirits were high. Naturally, he started off at a trot, but he quickly accelerated. He wore a wide smile as the wind struck him and the rain splattered against his face. Leaning forward, he was at a high level sprint in no time and there was no shortness of breath, no heaviness in his chest, no strain in his legs— he quite literally had a boundless supply of energy, a supernatural supply of energy.

He ran, he jumped, and in the rain he even lost his footing and slipped and tumbled a few times, but he never stopped moving. This was fast, faster than he'd ever imagined. His destination was Jezreel, the same place that Ahab's chariot left for several minutes before him.

The rain was coming down hard now, and Elijah started to lose his footing again. Avoiding a nasty face-plant in the mud, he slid forward and jumped, and then kept right on running. His arms and legs pumped like a machine and before he knew it he was actually coming up on Ahab's chariot. With a smile and a wave Elijah passed the chariot and the bewildered king who was barking orders at his driver.

Elijah came up to the city and ran right inside until someone hollered at him. "Elijah!" the stranger said, "Come in here and rest awhile! I heard the story about Mount Carmel; that's amazing."

Elijah thanked the man, came inside, and shared a meal with his family. Up to that point, it was the greatest day of Elijah's life: he had firsthand witnessed a miracle and a revival, had the hand of God endow him with supernatural speed for a run, and he even got to make fun of four hundred and fifty Baalite prophets for a few hours. The endorphins flowed through his bloodstream giving him a natural high. He felt great, and he felt hungry. His guests were more than happy to feed him and listen to his stories and jokes; they all talked late into the night and laughed together.

That night he slept the hardest that he could ever remember.

And then the morning came, and his whole body was sore. The endorphins that blocked the pain from his run were gone. "I feel like an old man!" he grunted to the little one of the house who was scampering by.

Elijah thanked the man and left. This time he wasn't running, he was walking. Every step hurt, just a little. Everything was stiff and sore and he stopped to stretch several times. He was tired. *Yesterday was a much better day than today,* he thought. He sat under a tree for rest and put his hands to his face, rubbing his eyes. Twisting, he tried to crack his back but to no avail.

"Elijah the Tishbite!" a man said, seeming to appear out of nowhere.

Elijah nearly jumped out of his skin. "What? Huh? Who are you?"

"Are you Elijah the Tishbite, prophet of Jehovah?" the man said in an incredibly loud and grating voice.

"Of course I'm Elijah, who else dresses like this?" Elijah said, as he rubbed his weary face again.

"Elijah the Tishbite, Prophet of Jehovah! Hearken unto me! Thus saith Queen Jezebel, the wife of King Ahab, High Prophetess and Priestess of Baal, Mediatrix of All Things Spiritual and Enlightened, Grand Poobahess of the Tolerant and Open-Minded Society of

Sacred Abortionists, Chieftess of the Foundation for Cosmetic Spackling of Wrinkled Women— OUCH!"

While still sitting under the tree, Elijah had reached over and hit the man across the ankles with his rod. "Enough! What's the old hag have to say?"

"She said she heard about what you did to her prophets," the man said. "And she says that she's going to make your life as the life of one of them by tomorrow."

"Is that so?" Elijah barked. "Well, tell her I said to come and get me!"

The man turned and walked away and Elijah snorted.

But then something happened inside of Elijah. You see, the day before was amazing, but so far this day had been pretty rotten. The day before he was high on the mountain and was receiving a blessing, but today was different. He was tired and sore and weary, and he hadn't even read the scriptures that morning and it was already afternoon. The sweet by-and-by of yesterday was gone, and he was in the dregs of the dirty now-and-now.

In spite of all the sarcasm and swagger that Elijah had, something else started to grip his heart. It was fear.

"That woman wants me dead, LORD," Elijah said.

God didn't say anything.

"I'm going to die," Elijah whispered.

God still didn't say anything. The physical symptoms of panic started to manifest themselves: Elijah could feel tightness in his chest, his hands began to tremble, and he began to sweat. With his fingers he pinched the sweat off his brow and stood up.

"I have to leave. I have to go," he said to himself. He dusted himself off and quickly started a new journey into the wilderness. This time he didn't run with joy and excitement. The carefree spirit of Elijah had vanished. He walked and he thought. He worried about tomorrow. He thought of all the different things that could possibly happen to him.

He felt very much alone.

Elijah went a day's journey into the wilderness trying to separate himself from society as much as he could. He was exhausted from the inside out. This was a very unusual experience for Elijah. The worry and fear was eating him up and wearing him out.

He came upon a juniper tree and sat down under it. The tears made their way out as he rested there, staring at the ground in front of him. He lay down and closed his eyes, praying as he drifted off to sleep. "It's enough LORD, no more. Please take away my life. I'm not any better than my fathers."

The LORD, once again, didn't say anything. Of course there were plenty of things he could have said, but he didn't say anything. He just let Elijah fall asleep.

Three hours later Elijah felt something touch his shoulder. When he opened his eyes he saw a pitcher of water and behind that a small cake warming over some coals.

"Arise and eat," an angel said to him. Elijah looked up and saw him. He looked like any other man, but Elijah knew he was an angel.

"Arise and eat because the journey is too great for thee," the angel said again.

"What journey? Where am I supposed to go? Listen, I'm tired and I'd rather just die if it's all the same to you—"

But before Elijah could finish the angel vanished. Elijah did as he was told and ate the food, and felt physically refreshed. And then he walked and he walked and he walked, all the way to Mount Sinai. Then he climbed it, without eating anything. He spent forty days and forty nights on this journey, all without eating. Absorbed in his own thoughts, he never considered the magnitude of what he was doing; or if in another time, the company he kept.

Looking for shelter, Elijah came upon a cave and went inside of it. It was cold and damp; Elijah found a corner to sit down again. And now after all of this, God was going to speak to him.

"What are you doing here, Elijah?"

Elijah's eye's widened suddenly. "I have been very jealous for the LORD God of hosts: for the children of Israel have forsaken thy covenant, thrown down thine altars, and slain thy prophets with the sword; and I, even I only, am left; and they seek my life, to take it away."

There was silence for just a few moments, and then God spoke again. "Go and stand on the mount, Elijah. I am going to pass by."

Elijah stood up and walked to the edge of the cave and for some reason he almost expected to see the back parts of God. Instead Elijah was pushed back as an enormous gust of wind struck him. The roar of the wind was deafening; Elijah gazed out from the edge and watched rocks break off and roll down the mountain.

"LORD?" Elijah cried out into the noise of the wind. "Are you there, LORD?"

But there was no answer. The ground shook and more rocks began to tear loose. Elijah kept crying out, but there wasn't any answer.

Then the entire mountainside across from Elijah was suddenly on fire. The sudden heat caused Elijah to step back and cover his face. He screamed once again for the LORD, but there was no answer.

And then everything stopped. The mount wasn't burning, in fact it looked like it had never been on fire before. There was no wind, everything was complete silence.

Then there was a very, very quiet voice.

"Elijah, what are you doing here?"

Then Elijah responded by saying the same thing he had five minutes ago. "I have been very jealous for the LORD God of hosts: because the children of Israel have forsaken thy covenant, thrown down thine altars, and slain thy prophets with the sword; and I, even I only, am left; and they seek my life, to take it away."

The LORD didn't chide Elijah, or go into all the reasons why Elijah was wrong, instead he just gave him a job to do. God knew that Elijah would never actually be able to get around to finishing the job he was about to give him, but that didn't matter. The important thing was Elijah needed something to do now, and the LORD knew it.

After giving him the instructions that would set his mind right, God finished up by reminding Elijah that he wasn't alone. He mentioned someone by the name of

Elisha, and then he said, "Yet I have left me seven thousand in Israel, all the knees which have not bowed unto Baal, and every mouth which hath not kissed him."

Elijah's mind had been renewed, and his heart had been refreshed. He descended the mountain and followed the path the LORD had told him to follow. He was looking for Elisha.

Passing by Elisha, he simply tossed his mantle upon him and kept right on walking.

"What's this?" Elisha said in surprise. "You're Elijah! Wait! I've always wanted to meet you! The LORD said I'm supposed to follow you!"

Elijah was back to his old self again. "Then get the lead out, boy, and let's go."

"Wait, wait!" Elisha said, wide-eyed and breathless as he ran to catch up. "Let me go and say goodbye to my mother and father! Then I'll follow you!"

Elijah kept on walking. "Do what you got to do, son. You don't need my permission, but I'm not stopping for anyone."

Elisha ran back home, said goodbye, had a meal with his parents, and then ran off to find Elijah again. Fortunately God had more grace with Elisha than Elijah did, and he guided him to where he found Elijah again.

When he found him later that evening, he was sitting on a stump and had scrolls and scraps of paper everywhere. He was feverishly working on something.

"I'm here!" Elisha said with a big smile.

"Congratulations," Elijah said.

"What are we going do?" Elisha said, with a hop in his step and a youthful melody in his voice.

"We," Elijah said, "are going to make a school. We are going to turn this nation around and train the seven thousand that haven't bowed the knee to Baal. We are going to make a scripture institute and call it the sons of the prophets."

Elisha smiled and reached down and took the scroll from Elijah. "You talk, I'll write. How's that sound to you?"

Elijah smiled. "Glad you figured out how to make yourself useful, son."

Chapter Thirty-Nine

"Then said he, These *are* the two anointed ones, that stand by the Lord of the whole earth."
Zechariah 4:14

896 B.C. Samaria

The years passed and some things changed in Israel. Elijah and Elisha raised up some fiery preachers who were fearless and dedicated to the LORD. The two men were an amazing team. Elijah gave them the orneriness they needed and Elisha helped them with the rest. About half of the nation repented, and amazingly enough even King Ahab repented for a brief period of time. Jezebel no longer had free reign to force her Baalite religion on the people as before.

There was constant war between Israel and Syria. Ahab was a mighty man of war and led his armies to victory many times. However, Ahab fell back into his old ways and forsook the LORD again. He dragged the king of Judah, Jehoshaphat, into the war with him.

Before going into the battle both of the kings were warned by one of the sons of the prophets, Micaiah, that this battle would spell the end of Ahab. Micaiah was much more like Elijah than Elisha, and Jezebel had pulled some strings to put the preacher in jail. But Micaiah was right, and Ahab was killed in battle and Jezebel died a violent death shortly thereafter.

All this led to Ahab's son, Ahaziah, taking the throne of the northern kingdom of Israel. Sadly, Ahab's brief period of repentance was not enough to change what his son was to become: a man far worse than his father. The country grew darker again as Baalism was reinforced throughout.

But Ahaziah became sick, and so he sent messengers to the land of Ekron to enquire of Baalzebub whether or not he was to recover. Apparently his version of Baal worship left him a little bit wanting in the foretelling part.

Ahaziah was rudely awakened when the door to his bedroom swung open.

"Your Majesty the king!" the servants said.

Ahaziah rubbed his head and sat up. "You could have knocked, you know."

The leader stepped forward. "Begging your apoligies, Your Majesty, but the strangest thing happened on the way to Ekron, and we assumed you'd want to know right away."

"Go on," Ahaziah said impatiently.

"Well, we were traveling down the road when all of a sudden some lunatic jumped out into the middle of the road and yelled boo at us."

Ahaziah scowled. "He yelled boo?"

"Yes, he yelled boo!"

"Okay, and you woke me up for this?"

"No," the man said. "Sorry, no, he gave us a message. He asked if you had sent messengers to Ekron because there's no God here. Then he said because you asked after Baalzebub instead of Jehovah you would die."

Ahaziah turned pale. "I see. What kind of man did you say this was?"

"Oh, I don't think it's anything to be alarmed over, king."

"Answer the question!" Ahaziah screamed. Then coughing he fell back into his bed, blood coming out the corner of his mouth. When the coughing spell ended, the man continued.

"Sorry, Your Majesty. This man was very hairy, and dressed in leather."

Ahaziah whispered something in return.

"What's that?" the messenger said.

"I said it's Elijah! It's that cursed Elijah back to trouble us again! He plagued my father and mother, and now he's after me!"

"I'm sorry my king, what are your orders?" the man said.

"Go and get him. Bring him to me now," the king said.

* * *

The scouts searched the land of Israel for Elijah, and this time it didn't take long to find him. Elijah wasn't scared of anyone trying to kill him, and he wasn't trying to hide by a river or anything. You see, many people falsely claim not to care, but in Elijah's case he really didn't care anymore. He loved the LORD; he loved God's people, and he loved to preach; but for better or worse, he didn't care about anything or anyone else, including his own personal safety.

And so a squad of fifty men came to apprehend Elijah and bring him to the king. He sat under a tree on the top of a hill, eating an apple. As the men approached the hill they mumbled about the tediousness of the task and how they wanted some real action.

"All right, you man of God," the captain said with sarcasm as the other men chuckled. "We can do this the easy way or the hard way. Come on down and let's go."

"If I be a man of God," Elijah said, and then interrupted himself by taking a bite from the apple.

He cleared his throat. "As I was saying, if I be a man of God, then let fire fall down from heaven and burn you guys up."

And the fire fell. It was fast and sudden and bright. Elijah never bothered to look; he just took another bite from his apple.

Another group of soldiers arrived. This time no one was laughing as they marched forward to the base of the hill. A blackened and charred skull was crushed under the heavy foot of the captain as he stepped forward.

"How dare you, Elijah! I knew these men! They had families! They were devout and religious men! They were fathers and sons! You're no man of God! You're a fraud! You're a bigot and narrow-minded hater! Hater, hater, hater, hater! How could you—"

He was interrupted by a small object that caught his attention as it rolled down the hill. It rolled, hit a rock and jumped up, and rolled some more, and then finally stopped at his foot.

It was an apple core.

"Elijah!" the captain said with anger and determination in his voice. "O man of God! You have to obey the king, and the king hath said for you to come down!"

Now most people, quite naturally, would try to defend themselves against such an onslaught of negative comments made against them. Perhaps they'd point to the inconsistencies of the statements made, such as the fact that when Baalism was the dominant religion worshipers of Jehovah had to flee for their lives. Another glaring inconsistency to ponder was that the other fifty soldiers, the fathers and sons, had also killed other fathers and sons and perhaps just received what they had coming to them. Or finally Elijah could have dodged the indictments by blaming God for roasting them, claiming that God made the decision to fry them probably because they were Baalites who just deserved it.

But, once again, this was Elijah. And Elijah just didn't care.

"If I be a man of God, then let fire fall down from heaven and consume thee and thy fifty!"

And that was that. Now the bones of a *hundred* soldiers lay at the bottom of the hill.

When the third captain came, his tone was much different. His men stood a fair distance from him, as he approached the base of the hill alone. He fell to his knees and cried out to Elijah, "O man of God, I pray thee, let my life, and the life of these fifty of thy servants, be precious in thy sight."

About that time an angel tapped Elijah on the shoulder. "Don't ask to burn these ones. Go ahead and go with them."

"All right!" Elijah hollered down to him. "I'm coming down!

Elijah let the men take him to the king, and he gave the king the bad news in person. Ahaziah took it as well as could be expected. Elijah's reputation had preceded him, and he knew there was no point in trying to fight it.

It was the last message Elijah gave to a king. A few weeks later he was to be raptured. It wasn't a surprise to anyone, especially Elisha. Everyone that ran into Elisha was constantly reminding him of the soon fate of his master. On the day that the miracle was to occur, Elisha refused to leave his side.

"Now listen up," Elijah said. "I need you to stay here while I head on over to Jordan."

Elisha smiled. "I don't know why you keep doing this, master, but I'm not leaving you no matter what."

"Oh really? You don't have to run on home to give out some goodbye kisses first?"

The fifty sons of the prophets that stood nearby chuckled until Elisha shot them a glare.

"That was a long time ago," Elisha said, only mildly embarrassed. "As the LORD liveth, and as thy soul liveth, I will not leave thee."

Elijah looked at Elisha. His tanned face didn't look a year over forty years old, and he was just as strong as he ever was before. He looked over at the fifty fire-breathing preacher boys, all standing at attention before the two men.

"You boys listen to me," Elijah said. "You follow Elisha's lead. I'll be leaving, and he's taking my place. You boys wouldn't be here if it weren't for him; he's clean as a hound's tooth, and knows the word better than anyone I know."

His eyes started to water up, and his voice cracked a little. "I'm proud of you boys. You've got grit."

At that point several of the preacher boys started to cry. They couldn't help it; no one had ever seen Elijah actually tear up before.

"No don't start weeping in your soup for me; you've got a job to do. If you want me to stay proud of you, then you'll finish the job. You'll finish the job; you'll finish it clean, and you'll finish it with joy."

Elijah looked at them as they all quickly wiped their tears away. There was a moment of silence. "Amen?" Elijah said.

"Amen!" they all echoed.

"All right!" Elijah said and turned and mumbled to Elisha, "I'm glad that's over with, I don't know how much more of that I could—"

And Elisha was crying too. Elijah threw his hands up in the air, "You bunch of babies! How we going to turn this world upside down for the LORD with a bunch of overgrown—"

He was suddenly interrupted as Elisha grabbed him and hugged him; at the same time the other fifty men started making their way to embrace him. He made no effort to resist, and he even let a few tears out along the way.

"You men stay here while Elisha and I head over to Jordan."

The two men walked together over to the water, and Elisha wiped his tears away. Reaching the riverbank, Elijah smiled to Elisha and said, "Watch this."

He quickly slipped the mantle off from his shoulder and slapped the water. Suddenly, as if a giant invisible hand was damming water, it began to pile up on one side of the river. On the other side all of the water continued to flow downstream as normal, only all the moisture from the wet ground was sucked out as well, leaving the ground perfectly dry.

Elisha looked at the dry ground in amazement, then back at the fifty sons of the prophets.

"Come on Sunshine, I got somewhere to be and it ain't here," Elijah said. They walked across the riverbed and as they came to the other side Elijah spoke again. "Son, is there anything you want from me before I leave?"

"Elijah," Elisha said, straightening himself up to look the man in the eye. "You've always been a sort of hero to me. And I'm going to do my best to continue what you've left me. This nation isn't going to go down on my watch, if I can help it. But I'm going to need a lot of strength to do that. The people are getting jaded to the word and paganism is on the rise again."

"So what can I do for you, son?" Elijah said.

Elisha looked away for a moment, then back at Elijah. "I pray thee; let a double portion of thy spirit be upon me."

Elijah held his chin in thought, and as he did all the water that had been piling up suddenly collapsed and the Jordan river began to flow normally again. "There's no success without a successor. You're asking a hard thing, but if you see me when I go, you'll get it."

As they walked, they shared memories of the past and Elisha ran scenario after scenario gleaning every last bit of wisdom he could from the man. Without warning, the weather changed dramatically and coldness filled the air as if it were going to rain.

Elijah stopped and smiled at Elisha, "You might want to step back."

The hair on the back of Elisha's neck stood up, and he felt a sudden chill. Elijah looked to the sky, and Elisha's gaze followed to the giant black cloud above them. A stream of light began to rupture through and then it burst open. The clouds parted and a brilliant white chariot alive with the fire of God Almighty and pulled by ten horses of fire fell through the sky towards them. Elisha took several steps back and tripped over something as the flaming chariot parted the two of them.

The chariot circled Elijah as he stood there gazing in the heavens. He hadn't moved the entire time. Elisha looked at him, then looked up and saw nothing, then looked back at Elijah. Round and round the chariot flew around Elijah until he started to rise into the sky. In a moment he was gone.

Elisha just sat there, dazed. The wind died down, the leaves came to rest on the ground again. Sorrow filled his heart, and he buried his face in hands and sobbed. "My father, my father, the chariot of Israel, and the horsemen thereof." He wept there for a short while, and then something fell down in front of him.

It was the mantle.

Elisha picked up the mantle of the old prophet of God, walked over to the Jordan River, and raised it in the air.

"Where is the LORD God of Elijah?" he cried as he brought the mantle down and struck the water. To the shock and amazement of the fifty sons of the prophets, the water parted just as before and Elisha walked across to join them.

Throughout his life Elisha received the double portion of Elijah's power. He performed twice as many miracles as Elijah, and God blessed the work of Elisha and the sons of the prophets as their ministry grew.

As for Elijah, his story didn't end when he went to Heaven. At some point in his blissful time beyond the sunset he was ushered by Gabriel into a secluded room, a special compartment of sorts, within Heaven itself.

Within that room there was the last thing that Elijah would ever expect. Elijah may have expected golden angelic armament, or perhaps musical instruments, or maybe even some sort of equipment for horses or chariots. But that's not what Elijah saw. He saw a table, and on both sides of the table there was an angel standing guard, and on that table there was the body of a man.

Gabriel spoke to the angels. "Leave us for a moment."

Then he turned to Elijah. "Do you know who that is?"

"No,"

"You don't recognize him?"

"No,"

"That's the body of Moses," Gabriel said.

"I thought he'd be taller," Elijah said.

"Do you know why you're here?" Gabriel said.

"I'm actually mostly wondering where the rest of him is."

"His soul? It's in Paradise, just like the rest of them, other than Enoch of course," Gabriel said.

"I like Enoch. Did you take him up here too?" Elijah asked.

"Yes, but he said no. Well, actually he said he wanted to think about it, and then he said no."

"You have no idea how utterly confused I am about this whole thing," Elijah said.

"Moses is coming back one day, and he's going to die. God didn't give him a resurrection body because a resurrection body is immortal and can't die. Moses needs to die again, so we're keeping his body up here in the exact same condition it was before, and we need someone else to go down to earth with him and die with him. Later we, of course, join his body and soul back together again, but it won't be for awhile."

Elijah stared at Gabriel for a couple of awkward heartbeats. "So you're asking me to give all this up and go back down to that dirty old place and die as a martyr or something?"

"Yes," Gabriel said with a nod.

Elijah looked down and then back up at him. "I can't imagine why Enoch said no."

"You don't have to if you don't want to," Gabriel said.

Elijah just thought about it.

For a long time.

Chapter Forty

"Thou shalt not be afraid for the terror by night; *nor* for the arrow *that* flieth by day;"
Psalm 91:5

710 B.C. Jerusalem

While Elijah was considering his options, time was flying by on planet Earth. Roughly a hundred and fifty years had passed and it would seem that the work done by the school of the prophets had gone up in smoke. The nation of Israel, that is the ten northern tribes, had been captured and taken into captivity by the ancient but resurgent empire of Assyria. They had sinned in walking in the statutes of the heathen and the chastisement of the LORD was upon them.

The two remaining tribes, the kingdom of Judah, were hanging on by a thread. King Hezekiah lay prostrate upon the ground before the temple of the LORD. Weeping in prayer, he spread the letter across the ground.

"O LORD of hosts, God of Israel, that dwellest between the cherubims, thou art the God, even thou alone, of all the kingdoms of the earth: thou hast made heaven and earth.

Incline thine ear, O LORD, and hear; open thine eyes, O LORD, and see: and hear all the words of Sennacherib, which hath sent to reproach the living God."

The message from the enemy was clear: Jerusalem was to surrender or face the wrath of Assyria. The Assyrians were gruesome masters of brutality. Those who dared to challenge them wound up being skinned alive or skewered upon a stake, done so in such a meticulous manner in order to keep the victim writhing in agony for a long as possible.

Hezekiah's prayer continued. "Of a truth, LORD, the kings of Assyria have laid waste all the nations, and their countries,

And have cast their gods into the fire: for they were no gods, but the work of men's hands, wood and stone: therefore they have destroyed them.

Now therefore, O LORD our God, save us from his hand, that all the kingdoms of the earth may know that thou art the LORD, even thou only."

* * *

That night the massive army of Assyria was camped out for miles. The city of Jerusalem, less than fifty square miles, had been prepared as best as it could be. Under the command of the king, the springs outside the city had been blocked to deprive the Assyrians of water. New walls and towers had been built for defense. A massive underground tunnel had been built to supply the city with water.

Pure futility.

Over the camp of the Assyrian army, if one were watching from miles and miles away, a small beam of light could be seen as it flew from the heavens straight to the middle of the sleeping camp. The light hung suspended over the camp, then in a flash it shot to the ground.

Michael the archangel landed on the earth, his golden armour coursing with blue lightning. For a few brief moments the aura of his presence lightened the still sleeping camp. A living darkness began to slowly encroach upon the light, and Michael drew his sword.

"Whenever you're ready," a figure said from the darkness as dozens of gasping and snarling shadows began to envelop him. They came quickly, not giving the archangel much time to respond. Michael raised his sword skyward and sudden rush of yellowish-blue lightning cracked from the heavens and struck the tip of his blade. It surged through the sword and into his body as the brightness pushed the devils back. They fought through the pulsating light and continued to close in on the archangel.

As if he could take no more, Michael roared and plunged his blade into the ground. The lightning detonated and spread through the entire camp of the Assyrian army. The demons disintegrated, disappearing to parts unknown. The vast majority of the Assyrian camp died instantly. Michael reached for his sword as the smoke cleared away and through the mist he saw the image he had been expecting.

It was a great red dragon, that is to say, the great red dragon. The dragon lowered the wing he had held up to shield himself and glared at Michael with eyes of fire.

"Smite my army, will you? Vanquish my devils?" he said as he approached, every step shaking the ground. Michael pulled his sword from the ground and held it in front of him.

The dragon laughed as he continued to stomp forward. "Did Jehovah send you to vanquish me as well?"

"No," Michael said as he tightened the grip on his sword.

"Very well then," the dragon said. His shape quickly changed as he continued to move forward, morphing into the image of a man. "I suppose we can discuss what just happened."

"Hezekiah prayed and the LORD empowered me to slay these soldiers, what is there to talk about?" Michael asked.

"Yes, definitely a setback, but certainly there's no finality to be found here."

"Jehovah has protected his people once again," Michael said, already regretting the fact that he was in this conversation. "The seed will arrive and bruise your head, and then shall the end come."

"Jehovah has protected his people once again," Satan repeated to himself a few times as he looked at the ground for a brief moment.

The he paused, and looked back at Michael. "Are those of Israel not his people as well?"

"Yes, they are," Michael said. "But the seed is to come thr—"

"If the ten northern tribes are his people then why didn't he protect them? Why did they suffer and die? Why were they taken from their homeland?"

"Because they forsook the LORD, they are in chastisement."

"And when the blessed and chosen of Judah do the same, then what?"

"That's the LORD's doing."

"He'll banish them from the promised land too!" Satan laughed. "He just can't help it! Oh, Michael, can't you see? Round and round we will forever go until there's simply nothing left of this world for your dear sweet redeemer to redeem! And then, there will be just you and me. He'll abandon this world, and it will be mine again."

Michael just looked at him.

Satan smiled. "Want in with me? I'll let you have half."

"My work here is done," Michael said as he put his sword in its sheath, gave the devil one last look, and shot upwards to the third heaven.

Chapter Forty-One

"Bring forth therefore fruits worthy of repentance, and begin not to say within yourselves, We have Abraham to *our* father: for I say unto you, That God is able of these stones to raise up children unto Abraham."
Luke 3:8

599 B.C. Jerusalem

Jeremiah was about fifty years old. His hair was thin, his face was wrinkled, but he still stood with his back straight and tall. He'd seen a lot in those fifty years in the land of Judah. He saw a young king, Josiah, turn the nation back to God. Josiah destroyed the idols, wept over the word of God, and repaired the temple. Josiah broke the altar of Jeroboam and burned his bones to ash on it, just like the young prophet who died had said he would. Josiah enacted fifty-two reforms and brought about the greatest revival the nation of Judah had ever seen. Jeremiah had seen some wonderful things.

But things had changed. Jeremiah saw Josiah, perhaps the last hope for Judah, die in battle. The Babylonian empire was on the rise, and Josiah was trying to help the Babylonians by keeping the Egyptians from reinforcing Assyria. Josiah believed that if he could help the stronger nation that perhaps he could maintain Judah's freedom. Pharoah Necho rightly asked *what have I to do with thee, thou king of Judah?* Josiah had involved himself in an external political matter without the consent of God, and he died because of it.

The morality of the nation went into a freefall from that point. Babylon grew stronger and had no regard for Judah's attempt at assistance. Because of the reckless moment of another good king two hundred years earlier, they had seen the beauty of Judah and the gold of Solomon's temple. The city was now in siege by the king of Babylon.

Two amazingly good kings, two reckless moments separated by two hundred years, and now complete failure. Jeremiah, the weeping prophet, was left to try and salvage the nation. Jeremiah lived most of his life in heartbreak for Judah, not because he saw it in the shambles it was in, but because in his lifetime he saw it go from the greatest revival ever to complete apostasy. No other nation had fallen so far, so fast.

He stood on a street corner and he preached. "You need to give it up, people. God hasn't forsaken you, but the kingdom is finished. Judah will be taken by Nebuchadnezzar, and when he enters the city he will not spare the life of mother or child! Babylon will take Jerusalem and burn it to the ground!"

About that time some scoffer would holler out, "But what if we repent? What if we return to the LORD?"

"You don't want to repent," Jeremiah would call back. "Even if you did, it's still too late. If you want to live, you need to surrender to the king of Babylon. If you leave the city and surrender to him, then you'll live. If you stay and fight, you'll die."

The nationalistic pride of the people always threw them into a frenzy at this point. "We be Hebrews! We'd rather die than surrender to the gentile dogs!"

Jeremiah nodded. He had heard it all before. Every day it was the same thing. "Then die you shall, oh prideful Judean. Die you shall."

"The Queen of Heaven will deliver us!" another would cry out.

"That's right," his companion would echo. "The Queen of Heaven—why, we baked caked to the Queen of Heaven and she increased our crops! She's real; she'll deliver us!"

Jeremiah, with the shackles still on his feet and hands, got on his knees before the cowardly king. He was thin and tired and weary from being in prison. The bruises still marked his face from how he had been mistreated. "I'm begging you. If you love your people and you want to save their lives, then surrender to the king of Babylon."

The king took a deep breath. "But my advisors! They tell me I can't! They say that all the people will turn against me. They mock anyone who suggests surrender. I don't want to be mocked, Jeremiah! I already have too much stress as it is. I just can't handle the criticism I'll get if I try to take a stand on this."

"You'll die, and it will only be by the mercy of God if they don't all die, king."

"No, there has to be another way. There's just has to be another way."

Jeremiah was tired, frustrated, and grief-stricken. Right there on his knees, he simply put his face in his hands and he wept. There was nothing else to do or to say.

And Jeremiah was taken back to prison.

Chapter Forty-Two

"Then Simon Peter answered him, Lord, to whom shall we go? thou hast the words of eternal life."
John 6:68

"Wake up, Jeremiah," the guards said as they jangled the keys outside the prison bars.

Jeremiah wasn't asleep. He couldn't sleep. He'd been praying night and day since he was in prison. But there was no point in explaining that to these men.

"You're moving up in the world, Jeremiah!" one of them said.

"Yeah, you've got a real promotion heading your way!" the other laughed. The reached in and jerked the prophet into the hallway with them.

"Where are we headed now?" Jeremiah asked as they shoved him down the hallway.

"Oh, well, we're just following the king's orders. Apparently the council has really taken to you and convinced the king to put you in a special quarters within the prison."

They shoved Jeremiah against the wall, opened a rusty old door with a creak and then shoved him in another room. A room with a hole in the floor.

"Apparently the king doesn't have the guts to put you to death, so he's just hoping you'll die in prison," one of the guards said. "Now get in the bucket."

Jeremiah looked over, and saw a large bucket next to the hole. He looked back at the guards for a moment.

They laughed. "Oh c'mon Jeremiah. You're going down in that dungeon one way or another. Don't make us throw you down there."

Jeremiah crawled into the bucket and they lowered him down. The stone walls of the tube looked damp and moldy, and when bucket struck the ground Jeremiah fell out. He was on his hands and knees now; he was hurting, and starving. Everyone was starving; the whole city was starving. He was just out of the way.

The men laughed and called down to him. "Serves you right, Jeremiah! If you could have just learned to shut your mouth and keep your opinions to yourself, you wouldn't be in this situation!"

They pulled the bucket back up and closed the door over the top of the hole. It was made of metal bars, and so some light trickled down to where Jeremiah was weeping. As he cried and prayed, he noticed that the ground beneath him was soft and marshy, and the he sunk into the mud of the floor.

Jeremiah pushed himself up off the ground and stood up. He had filth all over him. "Oh LORD, what am I doing here? How is this part of your plan?"

He tried to get the mud and filth off his hands by wiping them on the walls. He was cold, and found a little wooden bench.

"Thank you, LORD, for this bench," he said.

Are you going to resign the ministry again, Jeremiah? the LORD said.

Jeremiah sighed, and leaned against the wall. "No, LORD, not this time. Retirement just isn't in my nature. You know I just have to preach; it's in my blood."

Some of those country preachers call that the can't-help-its, the LORD replied.

Jeremiah smiled, and hugged himself. It was cold. "I suppose so, LORD."

Why don't you quit, Jeremiah?

"There's nothing better to do. I don't say that flippantly; I mean it. I'd be suffering if I didn't serve you, so I might as well do something worthwhile."

It won't always be this way.

How much longer, LORD?"

I'm not done with you yet, Jeremiah. You won't be here long. This too shall pass.

The conversation went on such a long time that Jeremiah lost track. He had sweet fellowship with the LORD down in the pit. It was the last thing anyone would have expected, but being helpless and in a pit alone with the LORD was just what he needed.

The door opened above him and a voice called out. "Okay Jeremiah, time to come out! The king changed his mind—again."

The bucket came down, Jeremiah came back up, and they took him off to get cleaned up and appear once again before the king. Jeremiah was encouraged to meet the man, an Ethiopian eunuch, who was responsible for talking the king into freeing him.

Unfortunately, but certainly not unexpectedly, the king didn't change his position. When he was alone with Jeremiah, he would agree that they needed to surrender the city to Babylon; but when the advisors came in, he was always swayed into procrastinating.

Until the day came that the Babylonians entered Jerusalem.

Chapter Forty-Three

**"The crown is fallen *from* our head: woe unto us, that
we have sinned!"**
Lamentations 5:16

588 B.C. Jerusalem

The prophet put his pen to the paper and wrote.

How doth the city sit solitary, that was

full of people! how is she become as a widow! she that was great among the nations, and princess among the provinces, how is she become tributary!

She weepeth sore in the night, and her tears are on her cheeks: among all her lovers she hath none to comfort her: all her friends have dealt treacherously with her, they are become her enemies.

How hath the Lord covered the daughter of Zion with a cloud in his anger, and cast down from heaven unto the earth the beauty of Israel, and remembered not his footstool in the day of his anger!

The Lord hath swallowed up all the habitations of Jacob, and hath not pitied: he hath thrown down in his wrath the strong holds of the daughter of Judah; he hath brought them down to the ground: he hath polluted the kingdom and the princes thereof.

The elders of the daughter of Zion sit upon the ground, and keep silence: they have cast up dust upon their heads; they have girded themselves with sackcloth: the virgins of Jerusalem hang down their heads to the ground.

Mine eyes do fail with tears, my bowels are troubled, my liver is poured upon the earth, for the destruction of the daughter of my people; because the children and the sucklings swoon in the streets of the city.

The young and the old lie on the ground in the streets: my virgins and my young men are fallen by the sword; thou hast slain them in the day of thine anger; thou hast killed, and not pitied.

For the punishment of the iniquity of the daughter of my people is greater than the punishment of the sin of

Sodom, that was overthrown as in a moment, and no hands stayed on her.

Her Nazarites were purer than snow, they were whiter than milk, they were more ruddy in body than rubies, their polishing was of sapphire:

Their visage is blacker than a coal; they are not known in the streets: their skin cleaveth to their bones; it is withered, it is become like a stick.

They that be slain with the sword are better than they that be slain with hunger: for these pine away, stricken through for want of the fruits of the field.

The hands of the pitiful women have sodden their own children: they were their meat in the destruction of the daughter of my people.

The LORD hath accomplished his fury; he hath poured out his fierce anger, and hath kindled a fire in Zion, and it hath devoured the foundations thereof.

They ravished the women in Zion, and the maids in the cities of Judah.

Princes are hanged up by their hand: the faces of elders were not honoured.

They took the young men to grind, and the children fell under the wood.

The elders have ceased from the gate, the young men from their musick.

The joy of our heart is ceased; our dance is turned into mourning.

The crown is fallen from our head: woe unto us, that we have sinned!

But thou hast utterly rejected us; thou art very wroth against us.

Chapter Forty-Four

"Submit yourselves therefore to God. Resist the devil, and he will flee from you."
James 4:7

The day of invasion had come and gone. The people had been starving; in some cases they had been eating their own babies. The city was burned, and all the glory of Solomon's temple was taken. The indecisive king who tried to flee was forced to watch as his sons were murdered in front of him, and then he had his own eyes gouged out. Those that survived were allowed to stay under the occupation of a puppet government set up by Babylon.

All the atrocities that could be imagined happened to the LORD's people, and Jeremiah had just finished writing about it in his Lamentations. He sat at an old wooden table in a room by himself, a candle his only source of light. His eyes were sore from crying, his shoulders trembled with grief. He set the pen down and rested his face in his hands.

He felt a coldness enter the room, and the hairs on his neck stood up for just a brief moment. Jeremiah didn't hear anything, but he felt it. It rattled around in his head. The oppression filled the room.

The adversary was here.

Hello, Jeremiah.

This wasn't Jeremiah's first experience with this, and it wasn't even his first experience with it today. He closed his eyes and prayed to the LORD, quoting Scripture.

"How sweet are thy words unto my taste! Yea, sweeter than honey to my mouth. Thy word is a lamp unto my feet and a light unto my path."

Yes, David's writings. What can you tell me about his children, his lineage?

Jeremiah rubbed his forehead. "Then will I stablish the throne of thy kingdom, according as I have covenanted with David thy father, saying, There shall not fail thee a man to be ruler in Israel."

Aw yes, but here we are, with no ruler in Israel. There is no Israel. What can you tell me about that?

"But if ye turn away, and forsake my statutes and my commandments, which I have set before you, and shall go and serve other gods, and worship them;   Then will I pluck them up by the roots out of my land which I have given them; and this house, which I have sanctified for my name, will I cast out of my sight, and will make it to be a proverb and a byword among all nations."

Well, that only makes sense. You have to behave to get the goodies. By the way, you know your scriptures very well Jeremiah, you should be proud of yourself.

Jeremiah sighed in frustration. "But we are all as an unclean thing, and all our righteousnesses are as filthy rags; and we all do fade as a leaf; and our iniquities, like the wind, have taken us away."

Smart and humble! And quoting Isaiah! I bet you would have loved to live with Isaiah, to see the deliverance of God and not a pathetic king who couldn't make a decision to save his own life, let alone the lives of his people.

That threw Jeremiah off. "I would have loved to live back then."

Oh, don't feel too sorry for yourself; you had some good times back in the day.

"Yes. Josiah. I miss those days. There was real revival."

It sure isn't as it used to be, is it?

"No, it's not."

For the next few hours the disappointing thoughts of yesteryear plagued the weary prophet. He tried to sleep to escape it, but it wouldn't leave him alone.

Let's talk about Jeconiah. He was the last king of Judah, you know.

"No, he wasn't. Why after him was—"

Oh come now, you know your own scriptures better than that. Look at what you wrote, Jeremiah.

A rush of panic came over Jeremiah. He felt hasty, nervous, and incredibly uncomfortable. As if there was something he knew but forgot, and desperately needed to remember. He began to rifle through his own writings, searching for anything he could about the king Jeconiah. He knew who Jeconiah was, of course. He was the king right before Zedekiah, and it was Zedekiah who couldn't decide to give the city to Nebuchnezzar.

But what was so special about Jeconiah that was bothering him? Why did he have to keep looking into it? Did he really want to find out?

And then he came across it. Right there in his own writings. It took his breath away.

"I can't believe it."

Oh, I've seen it all the time. Isaiah, Micah, Habakkuk, Joel... they all wrote things that they had no idea what they were writing, until later.

"I can't . . . no, this can't be."

It is. The end. I win, you lose.

Jeremiah's fingers went over the words, inspired words that he had written.

"Is this man Coniah a despised broken idol? Is he a vessel wherein is no pleasure? Wherefore are they cast out, he and his seed, and are cast into a land which they know not?"

Yes, in plainer words, God was put out with Jeconiah so much that he changed his name. Keep on reading, the best is yet to come.

"O earth, earth, earth, hear the word of the LORD."

Yes, whatever God's about to say now is so important that he wants everyone to hear it.

"Thus saith the LORD, Write ye this man childless, a man that shall not prosper in his days: for no man of his seed shall prosper, sitting upon the throne of David, and ruling any more in Judah."

There it is! Game over! God cursed the precious and blessed line of Judah! You know what that means, right?

Jeremiah repeated the words. "No man of his seed shall prosper, sitting upon the throne—"

Exactly. Your Messiah is supposed to come through Judah, but now he can't. The shadow of the king is moving away from you, not towards you! I am the god of this world; the earth is the devil's and the fullness thereof, my dear lonely and tired prophet.

You are in the minority!

You are weak!

Your days are numbered!

Your messiah will never come, and I will sift your people as wheat!

His mind was spinning at this revelation. The attacks were merciless.

The truth is you're a fool and a failure, Jeremiah! You never won a single convert.

"But what about—"

They were all following Jehovah from back in the glory days of Josiah.

You are a failure.

No one listens to your preaching.

No one will ever read your writings.

"Oh, God, help me, please," Jeremiah said, but the attacks didn't stop. Then through the fog and the darkness the weeping prophet was drawn back to the Scriptures.

Back to his own writings.

The attacks kept coming. Jeremiah was franticly searching for something, anything. Through the blurry vision of his own tears he could barely read.

He wiped his eyes again and again. He put his fingers on a passage.

"Thus saith the LORD; If ye can break my covenant of the day, and my covenant of the night, and that there should not be day and night in their season;

"Then may also my covenant be broken with David my servant, that he should not have a son to reign upon his throne; and with the Levites the priests, my ministers."

The attacks stopped, just for a moment.

That's a contradiction.

"Last time I checked the sun came up this morning. This passage makes a lot more sense than that other one."

It's a contradiction. God cursed the line, that is clear. The seed is cursed! There will be no messiah! It doesn't make sense!

"It doesn't have to make sense. I trust God to keep his promises whether I understand it all or not."

Jeremiah wiped his eyes again. He turned to other passages. They all repeated the same promise, over and over again.

They don't matter. They've been destroyed by the fact that the seed is cursed. Your messiah is of the line of Judah.

"I don't have to understand it all; I just need to believe what he wrote. I trust God however he's going to work it out."

The attacks stopped for good. Jeremiah had read the word, believed the word, submitted to God, and resisted the devil. He looked down at what he'd finished writing several hours earlier, and he felt hope, peace, and the presence of God.

This I recall to my mind, therefore have I hope.

It is of the LORD'S mercies that we are not consumed, because his compassions fail not.

They are new every morning: great is thy faithfulness.

The LORD is my portion, saith my soul; therefore will I hope in him.

END OF BOOK TWO

Epilogue

115 years earlier, Jerusalem

The legendary prophet Isaiah had literally been stopped in his tracks and sent back to the home of Hezekiah. The great king of Judah lay sick and dying in his bed, but God had heard his prayer and granted him another fifteen years of life.

"Thank-you, my old friend," Hezekiah said, brushing the tears from his eyes. He reached for Isaiah's hands and grabbed them. "We sure have been through a lot, haven't we?"

Isaiah smiled as he stood by the king. "Yes we have, and it looks like we'll have another fifteen years."

Hezekiah sat up quickly, all vestiges of royal dignity gone at the exciting news of life. "What do they hold? You're the prophet of the LORD, what do those days hold?"

Isaiah looked away, then back again. "Are you certain you wish to know?"

Hezekiah laughed and slapped the bed. "Of course I do!"

Isaiah's face hardened. "Your Majesty, the future of Judah is calamity, darkness, and destruction. I can't see it all at this point, and I don't think it's going to happen anytime soon, but it's not good. I think we're going to lose the kingdom and our homeland."

Hezekiah's face turned pale. "Will it happen in my days?"

"At this point I'm not sure, but I do know one thing—" Isaiah paused midsentence.

"Go on, go on," the king said expectantly.

"The LORD'S servant will be a Gentile, his name will be Cyrus, and somehow, someway, he'll be the one to bring us back home."

When I Can Read My Title Clear
Isaac Watts, 1674-1748

1. When I can read my title clear
   To mansions in the skies,
   I bid farewell to every fear,
   And wipe my weeping eyes.
   I bid farewell to every fear,
   And wipe my weeping eyes.

2. Should earth against my soul engage,
   And fiery darts be hurled,
   Then I can smile at Satan's rage,
   And face a frowning world.
   Then I can smile at Satan's rage,
   And face a frowning world.

3. Let cares, like a wild deluge come,
   And storms of sorrow fall!
   May I but safely reach my home,
   My God, my heav'n, my All.
   May I but safely reach my home,
   My God, my heav'n, my All.

4. There shall I bathe my weary soul
   In seas of heav'nly rest,
   And not a wave of trouble roll
   Across my peaceful breast.
   And not a wave of trouble roll
   Across my peaceful breast.

Other books by
Rick and Melissa Schworer

15 Simple Steps
Losing Your Salvation

Faith and Finance:
Peace With or Without Prosperity

Roadmap Through Revelation